Int | AR

Interventions | **Adaptive Reuse**

Editors In Chief:
Markus Berger
Liliane Wong

Guest Editor:
Nick Heywood

Graphic Design Editor:
Ernesto Aparicio

Int|AR is an annual publication by the editors in chief: Markus Berger + Liliane Wong, and the Department of Interior Architecture, Rhode Island School of Design.

Members of the Advisory Board:

-Heinrich Hermann, Adjunct Faculty, RISD; Head of the Advisory Board, Co-Founder of Int|AR

-Uta Hassler, Chair of Historic Building Research and Conservation, ETH Zurich.

-Brian Kernaghan, Professor Emeritus of Interior Architecture, RISD

-Niklaus Kohler, Professor Emeritus, Karlsruhe Institute of Technology.

-Dietrich Neumann, Royce Family Professor for the History of Modern Architecture and Urban Studies at
 Brown University.

-Theodore H M Prudon, Professor of Historic Preservation, Columbia University; President of Docomomo USA.

-August Sarnitz, Professor, Akademie der Bildenden Künste, Wien.

-Friedrich St. Florian, Professor Emeritus of Architecture, RISD.

-Wilfried Wang, O'Neil Ford Centennial Professor in Architecture, University of Texas, Austin; Hoidn Wang Partner, Berlin.

Layout + Design_Xin Ma, Xiangyu Liu

Editorial + Communications Assistant_Anna Albrecht

Cover Design_Ernesto Aparicio, Liliane Wong

Cover Photo_*Rosa Parks House Project*, Berlin, Germany_Photograph by Fabia Mendoza

Inner Cover Photos_Markus Berger, Jeffrey Katz, Liliane Wong

Copyediting_Amy Doyle, Clara Halston

Printed by SYL, Barcelona

Distributed by Birkauser Verlag GmbH, Basel P.O. Box 44, 4009 Basel, Switzerland,

Part of Walter de Gruyter GmbH, Berlin/Boston

Int|AR Journal welcomes responses to articles in this issue and submissions of essays or projects for publication in future issues. All submitted materials are subject to editorial review. Please address feedback, inquiries, and other material to the Editors, Int|AR Journal, Department of Interior Architecture, Rhode Island School of Design, Two College Street, Providence, RI 02903 www.intar-journal.edu, email: INTARjournal@risd.edu

CONTENTS

LAID FLAT, NOW UPRIGHT

by NICK HEYWOOD

In composing this issue of the journal, we struggled with how to acknowledge the moment we are living through, which is for many an act of survival. Deceit, fraud, cruelty, division and war are represented on the front page of every newspaper the world over. Many of our leaders seem consumed by avarice, pride and vainglory, rather than the eternal question of how to live together equitably. Our era cannot take credit for this list of woes: each is represented in Ambrogio Lorenzetti's fresco for the council chamber of Siena, *The Effects of Bad Government*, painted in 1339.[1]

Add inertia and paralysis to the list above and you might have a more fitting portrait of our age. In the built environment, both microscopic and urbanistic, design interventions react to constraints of nature, clients, budgets, structural limits, and importantly the tone of the moment they are created. Faced with Lorenzetti's list, how can Interior Architecture contribute? In our call for papers, we quote George Bernard Shaw: "The possibilities are numerous once we decide to act and not to react." *Intervention as ACT* became shorthand in our conversation for work that rejects inertia and paralysis, running toward engagement with the most pressing issues of the day, be they formal, social, theoretical. We looked for heroes and heroic projects and many found us.

Against the tide of division, the work collected here attempts to bring us closer together. The belief that there is benefit to living equitably together with others has been forgotten and revived over and over across different cultures, but Western bias favors the Greeks and *synoikismos*, or "dwelling together" (a Heideggerian phrasing if ever there was) as an early expression.[2] King Theseus of Athens realized monsters were more easily conquered with help: living for shared good was best for all. Remembered for his ability to lead and join disparate people, his biography by Plutarch gives us the well-known philosophical paradox of Theseus' ship.

The ship on which Theseus sailed with the youths and returned in safety ... was preserved by the Athenians down to the time of Demetrius Phalereus. They took away the old timbers from time to time, and put new and sound ones in their places, so that the vessel became a standing illustration for the philosophers in the mooted question of growth, some declaring that it remained the same, others that it was not the same vessel.[3]

This was a living object. Athenians sailed the ship to the place they believed Theseus defeated the Minotaur -- it had to function, rowed through water over great distance, once annually for perhaps a thousand years. The journey was a pilgrimage that gave a sense of direct contact between citizens and the hero who brought them together. The last year the Athenians boarded, after not a splinter of the original remained, whose ship were they rowing? This story is told with the same dangling question but different players across most cultures: from an Indian Buddhist philosopher's knife to Washington's axe.[4] We have yet to answer the riddle that is Theseus' ship, just as we have yet to understand how to dwell together equitably.

How do you revisit heroism after the hero is gone? Rosa Parks took on an even greater monster than the Minotaur by going into battle against racism in the United States. She did so with strength and humility, and though she was celebrated as the mother of the Civil Rights Movement, though she did so much for so many, her famous act of refusal did little to improve her own life. Work was difficult to find. For long periods she lived in poverty. She never owned a home.[5] Bus No. 2857 is the star of the Henry Ford Museum of American Innovation and thousands of monuments have been erected to her memory, but where do you go to connect to the reality of the hero, alongside the act?

Theseus' ship was a mobile accessory to pilgrimage. Oddly it is the house where Parks slept and worked that fulfills this role, not bus No. 2857, which is permanently installed in a climate controlled museum setting.[6] *Everybody's House* (as show on cover and page 16) explores the peripatetic fate of Parks' brother's home, where she lived from 1957 to 1959. Parks knew this building when it was moored to the ground in Detroit, but it has been cut from context and moved to Berlin.

From Berlin it sailed to Providence, Rhode Island. The house's future is uncertain, as it will now be sold at auction to the highest bidder.

Composed of reconstituted fragments, the object where Parks took refuge loses flakes of paint and sometimes whole boards in transit; with each erection, it is a little less the place she once touched. What is this house? Is it even a house, or representative of a place, let alone a person? Is it a piece of sculpture? An object of veneration? What does it record, and what does dragging it across the world accomplish that leaving it in Detroit does not? How do we find the hero in this pile of timber, laid flat, now upright?

This issue of the journal collects heroism in myriad form, within unexpected sites and from uncharacteristic contributors. Here we have, among other interventions, the transformation of a radical printing press into an archive devoted to free speech in one of the most dangerous countries to be a journalist (p.62); an inclusive workplace cobbled together from materials bearing the scars of a total war that many believe constituted genocide (p.44); a homeless shelter that habituates dwellers through engagement in the process of redesigning and renovating the spaces they inhabit (p.68); an interview with the executive director of a community development corporation holding a portfolio of affordable housing projects valued at over $100 million (p.96); a case for digital graffiti as the vanguard spatial expression of civil protest (p.82); a meditation on architectural principles taught by a master mime used to mediate centuries of competing layers, discovering "through bodily attitudes, the past embodied in action" (p.52); a critical analysis of tactical urbanism that posits *lighter, quicker, cheaper* principles can be a vital tool of positive impact in imperiled communities, without displacing longtime residents (p.30); an argument that humanity so mightily impacts all of the earth that we are never not in an interior environment – that there is no longer an outside on earth (p.38).

The discipline of Interior Architecture is uniquely positioned to offer possible answers to the great question of how to live together equitably. Necessarily contextual, even if the decision is made to ignore context, every act of Interior Architecture grapples with competing narratives and determines which voices will be heard. Though the challenge is not always taken up, in each act of intervention there is an opportunity to correct, to set the record straight, to acknowledge. We believe the work presented here takes up the challenge of Intervention as ACT.

Providence, 2018

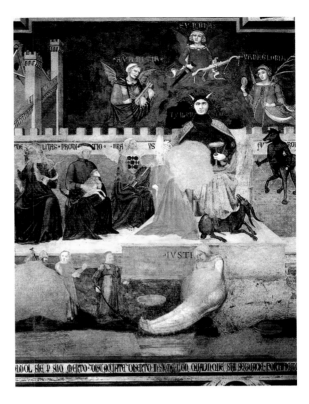

ENDNOTES:

1 Randolph Starn, *Ambrogio Lorenzetti: the Palazzo pubblico, Siena*. (New York: George Braziller, 1994)

2 Paul Rahe, *Republics Ancient and Modern*. (Chapel Hill and London: University of North Carolina Press, 1994) 323.

3 *Plutarch*. (translated by Bernadotte Perrin) (The Parallel Lives, Harvard University Press, Cambridge, 1914) 23:1.

4 Wendy Doniger, *The Implied Spider: Politics and Theology in Myth* (New York: Columbia University Press, 2010) 55.

5 Wall text, *The Rosa Parks House Project*, WaterFire Arts Center, Providence, RI.

6 The Henry Ford Museum of American Innovation. "What if I don't move to the back of the bus?" thehenryford.org. https://www.thehenryford.org/explore/stories-of-innovation/what-if/rosa-parks/ (accessed June 5th, 2018).

The Effects of Bad Government, Ambrogio Lorenzetti

FRAC Nord-Pas de Calais, Dunkirk, France

FARAWAY, SO CLOSE

FRAC NORD-PAS DE CALAIS: ON CLONING AND DUPLICATION

by STEFANO CORBO

"One egg, one embryo, one adult - normality. But a bokanovskified egg will bud, will proliferate, will divide. From eight to ninety-six buds, and every bud will grow into a perfectly formed embryo, and every embryo into a full-sized adult. Making ninety-six human beings grow where only one grew before. Progress." [1]

In his novel *Brave New World*, written in 1931, writer Aldous Huxley envisions a new model of society characterized by a peculiar process of cloning: the so-called Bokanovsky Process. Thanks to this fictional example of ectogenesis –imagined by Huxley as a method of human reproduction in which a fertilized egg can be split into as many as 96 embryos– any government or political power can program the number of humans, their behaviours and their actions. As in a futuristic Panopticon, social control is achieved through biological techniques and proto-genetic engineering. Ninety-six embryos, as pointed out in the novel, mean ninety-six identical machines: by creating and manipulating an artificial working class, the Power will assure itself an infinite prolongation of the status quo.

Whereas for Huxley cloning is a medium to preserve and instrumentalize social vigilance, in many recent design strategies cloning has served as a main tool to liberate architecture from programmatic pre-determinations, and at the same time, to establish renovated relationships between one or more buildings, their history and their functioning. Contrary to the scenario imagined by the English author –a world based on fear and control– architectural cloning can be an instrument of

7

freedom: freedom as a deliberate and active appropriation of space.

Cloning, in fact, is the interpretative key to describe one of Lacaton & Vassal's latest projects: the FRAC Nord-Pas de Calais in Dunkirk, France. A winning proposal of a competition held in 2009, the FRAC is a hybrid program, being an archive and an exhibition space at the same time. The starting point of this project is an old boat warehouse (Halle AP2), located in the port area and built in 1949. Rather than altering or modifying its formal characteristics, Lacaton & Vassal decided to duplicate the existing building, and to juxtapose to the Halle AP2 a new structure with the same dimensions and the same volumetry. If the warehouse is a massive concrete structure, its clone is a prefabricated and transparent envelope. Moreover, the whole program of the FRAC collections is condensed within the new construction: it provides 9,357 sqm. in addition to the 1,953 sqm. available in the old structure. By doing so, the Halle becomes a built void with no specific function: a flexible space, open to change and evolution. It can work as an extension of the FRAC activities, but can also have its own programmatic autonomy (concert, fairs, shows, etc.). Its life is separated but, at the same time, combined with that of the new structure.

The reuse of the Halle, inscribed within a wider process of redevelopment of the Dunkirk Port, makes the FRAC not simply a museum or an archive, but a collective catalyst: its abstract and symbolic character will function as a visual magnet in the post-industrial landscape of the port area. Second, its flexible program aims to attract the local community and at the same time to host international events. In the Halle AP2 no radical interventions or modifications have taken place: not only its structural integrity but also its raw, non-finite and industrial atmosphere has been preserved. Whereas the Halle is an enclosed vacuum to be colonized, its cloned structure follows the same compositive strategy that Lacaton & Vassal have been testing in one of their most successful projects: the Nantes School of Architecture building. In a similar way as in Nantes, the FRAC is conceived of as a vertical promenade that from the exterior takes the visitor up to a panoramic "belvedere": in other words, an example of vertical urbanism.

Elevators and a public staircase connect the different levels of the building. The new structure is a combination of different irregular spaces: café and exhibition rooms on the ground level, then administration areas, a double-height Forum, and the belvedere on the last floor. The Archive area, on the contrary, works as a repetitive stacking of levels: it is partially isolated and disconnected from the public circulation of the

Interior view from Halle AP2

building. A lift, located in the middle of the complex, will allow the transportation of the artworks from the ground floor to the three storey archive.

As seen before, the main difference between the old and new structure does not reside exclusively in their divergent spatial articulation, but mainly depends on their opposite materiality: in the new building, in fact, we can find some of those elements that made Lacaton & Vassal's projects so distinguished: exposed concrete, polycarbonate panels, greenhouse-like structures, etc. The choice of these materials responds only partially to aesthetic reasons: movable polycarbonate panels, for example, work as efficient thermodynamic devices as well. Thanks to their use, it is possible to control some climatic parameters within the building –temperature, humidity, pressure– and to optimize its energy behaviour. In many cases heating and air conditioning systems become unnecessary.

There is no indulgence for complex constructive models or expensive materials: Lacaton & Vassal are not interested in the phenomenological aspects of the design process. They don't work on the creation of atmospheres, and don't believe in the cathartic function of architecture. Their projects deal with time and performance.

In Dunkirk, apart from the idea of cloning as generative strategy, old and new structures are conventional constructions: their symbolic impact is not reached through a spectacularization of the design gestures, but through a method of intervention based on a strong conceptual component, which allows a connection of past and future, history and technology, memory and information.

For the materials employed and for some of the spatial and compositive techniques adopted in this project, one may say that the FRAC represents a coherent fragment in Lacaton & Vassal's long trajectory. Starting from the beginning of the nineties, in fact, the French firm has been experimenting with the evolutionary and adaptive character of their architectures. When working on existing structures, their projects turn into neutral palimpsests, capable of being customized according to the users' needs. In absorbing the lesson of Cedric Price, whose Fun Palace has always constituted one of their main sources of inspiration, Lacaton & Vassal question not only architecture and its traditional status, but also the role played by the architect in the design process. While Price explored in his projects the possibility of defining architecture through a constant practice of manipulation, based on cycles of assembly and destruction, Lacaton & Vassal address their efforts towards the progressive dismantlement of the architectural discipline in favour of its dilution within social and performative parameters.

Interior view from the Belvedere

these buildings, Lacaton & Vassal decided to transform them by proposing a radical extension of each apartment. New self-supporting structures are added on the old facade of the towers, in order to create terraces and loggias. These secondary parasitic structures, made of polycarbonate panels, do not offer only extra space, but at the same time work as thermal filter between the interior and the exterior, by allowing them to reach personal conditions of comfort.

Price's concern for temporality and spatial flexibility also influenced the project for the Palais de Tokyo, a modern Art Centre opened in 1937 and progressively abandoned after the completion of the Pompidou Centre in 1970's. Here Lacaton & Vassal applied some of their consolidated strategies: the use of exposed and raw materials −the original structure of the building was liberated by superfluous decorative strata and brought to light, the interest in time as a material of the project −patina is preserved and dramatized, the free colonization of the space. Contrary to many other galleries, in Palais de Tokyo the circulation pattern is not based on dictated routes. Visitors are free to invade the whole building: from the basement, converted into a sort of habitable cave, until the upper level exhibition spaces. The necessary technological apparatus displayed in the building is counterbalanced by its roughness, in the best of the neo-Brutalist tradition. In an analogous fashion to other projects from Lacaton & Vassal, Palais de Tokyo

As claimed by Price, architecture can only exist as a sequence of events, and not as a fixed point immerged into space: it should trigger appetites, desires, and inject them within the urban structure under the appearance of a collective Situationist game. The Fun Palace (1961), but also the InterAction Centre (1972-77), responded to this logic: if the idea of function can be subject to infinite potential modifications, and if form is free from tectonic and stereotomic constraints, architecture can be finally interpreted as a participatory or interactive machine, whose configuration depends on the dialogue between users and its components. At the same time, by assuming its ever-changing character, architecture will always contain a certain degree of indeterminacy, which will guarantee unexpected appropriations.

Consequently, in Cedric Price's opinion, even the role of the designer −a deus ex machina imposing his own worldview through the project− will disappear for good. Creativity, intended as a romantic vehicle of inspiration, is replaced by the precision and efficiency of new technological devices: well-known was Price's interest in cybernetics, game theory and information science. Porous, temporary and constantly evolving: that's how he envisioned his proposals, and projected architecture into a new dimension, where time and change shape an open notion of form. Similarly, in their projects Lacaton & Vassal express their perplexity for any sort of static, definitive and assertive approach to design.

In Bois le Prêtre Tower (Paris, 2011), or in Saint-Nazaire Housing project (2014-16), for example, the French duo confront Cedric Price's quest for adaptation and active participation. These two proposals shared a similar starting condition: an existing high-rise block built in the sixties-seventies. Instead of demolishing

TOP
Exterior view of FRAC Nord-Pas de Calais
BOTTOM
Nocturnal view of FRAC Nord-Pas de Calais

is an infrastructural support, that doesn't impose any functional or spatial decision, but that rather suggests a way to interact and engage with the artworks. Subtle or even invisible marks become thresholds or boundaries: ramps, variation in slope, doors and staircases.

Opposed to any modernist tradition, contemporary design is not anymore a process of tabula rasa. By recycling, modifying forms, re-interpreting existing messages, architecture engages with the strategic appropriation and manipulation of elements even proceeding from alien territories. At the same time, the traditional separation between different disciplines tends to evaporate, and architecture blurs into a constellation of innocent and ephemeral installations, extemporary episodes whose ultimate goal is simply to describe a certain temporary condition.

Against such a reassuring and innocuous vision stands the work of Lacaton & Vassal. As we have seen, when reusing existing structures, their projects are the paradigmatic expression of an alternative worldview: post-production can turn into an operative instrument of change and civic activism.

In Dunkirk, by preserving the spatial integrity of the old warehouse, Lacaton & Vassal emphasize again the unstable character of their architectures: in the same way as in Saint Nazaire's social housing tower, or in the Bois le Prêtre, the French office work on the idea of design as an open process. But if in the past any of

their projects of reuse implied a physical and material contact with the old structure, in Dunkirk their strategy becomes more abstract and conceptual.

At the same time, reuse is not articulated anymore as an operation of reaction to the physical, perceptive and spatial characteristics of an old building; nor is dictated by functional requirements or constraints. Through a project of reuse, Lacaton & Vassal apply for action: for a more participative and effective role that users can play in the making of their own environment, and by consequence, in the making of the city.

In other words, one may say that users become ecological tools: through their actions they can shape a new and sustainable modus vivendi.

ENDNOTES:
1 Aldous Huxley, *Brave New World* and *Brave New World Revisited* (New York: Harper Perennial, 2005), 17.

Palais de Tokyo, Paris, France: Interior view from the basement

TEMPORARY ACTS *THE DECORATORS*

by KRISTINA ANILANE AND LUIS SACRISTAN MURGA

With backgrounds in landscape architecture, interior architecture and psychology, The Decorators work on spatial design projects that aim to reconnect the physical elements of a place with its social dimension. They employ a methodology that builds on the social and cultural makeup of a site to create new experiences that can prompt interaction or shape communal memory. Their clients include local authorities, museums, curators and brands, and their work ranges from context-specific engagement strategies and public realm landscapes, to exhibition design and interactive interiors. Xavi Llarch Font and Carolina Caicedo, two of the four founders of The Decorators, discuss their approach and the importance of understanding how one's work will be used.

CAROLINA: We started working together in 2010, at the back of the financial crisis. There was a sense of wanting to act. Ridley's was our first project and opportunity to do something together. It came with the aspiration for us to test our methodology and our way of working together.

It was during the emergence of the pop-up in London, but the projects that were coming up in no way connected with the area, with the people that had been there before the neighbourhoods. We were interested

Ridley Road Market of Hackney, London. Analysis of this site led to the
creation of Ridley's, a self-sufficient temporary restaurant co-existing with
the market, the traders and neighbours

XAVI: The complex city needs more complex projects and not so many one-liners. Temporary architecture should be more complex than permanent architecture because it has the opportunity to test more radical thoughts. It's much more difficult to test new ideas in permanent interventions because no one is going to take the risk. If the brief would be about being there for 10 years, the conversation would be different.

Everyone sees the value of these temporary projects in a different way. Sometimes it is also a matter of scale. How can a project lasting three weeks, which is five by five square meters, be an influence for something that is a multimillion pound regeneration project?

As a practice, we like working with reality but also with fiction. And what we've been doing is telling a story. And the story might not be for everyone, it might be a story that we've made up. Some people will be happy and some people will be against it. But the fact that it is temporary allows for that kind of tension to happen and then it disappears again.

Being able to break down slightly those big masterplans, taking one of the elements and bringing it forward, activating it, performing in the public space with people who can come and have their say is valuable and it shows that those voices have an impact.

CAROLINA: Ridley's was self-initiated. We hadn't done any work before, and people see something in that project. That project is how we were contacted by Hackney Council and by the Greater London Authority, and because of that we've continued doing work.

Our projects are more about working on the ground, talking to people and finding out who they are, what a neighbourhood means to them, what a community means to them, and it's out of those big questions that our work develops. We know that we are there because change is coming. We probably don't have the answers. But in some way, we're trying through action to figure out ways of giving voice, of showing what's there already.

For example, in Ridley's the program of the restaurant came out of us walking around, talking to the traders, realizing that the site was overlooking market stores selling vegetables and the program of restaurant suddenly appeared. The program became this way of involving lots of different people who might not otherwise cross paths.

We're being contacted more and more by big architecture practices that are doing tenders and they see that they need to do engagement or consultation. They've seen the picture of Ridley's and they want one of those. And then it becomes a thing of replicating an image rather than what was more interesting about the project, which were the market traders that you met and how you got them involved in the project.

in developing temporary projects that directly spoke or connected to the social context rather than ignoring it.

In the case of Ridley's, we reflected on the site and through asking questions we finally gave form to the idea. By developing these questions we ended up inventing the brief. At the end, we created the book "Recipes for Food and Architecture" as a useful thing to pass to others who wanted to go through the same process.

In the UK, you can put up a temporary structure for 28 days. If it's up for more than 28 days then you have to apply for a planning application. This three-week period allowed us to activate the site without having to go through a more rigorous process of planning. But we were worried about the issue of legacy. Our question was: can a temporary project be used as a way of testing ideas for how cities could be? The way to extend the legacy of this project was by sharing the knowledge we got by doing.

Our ethos is that every place has something unique to celebrate. Our starting point is always finding out what is there, what is the specific culture of the place. Our interest in context is our way of trying to resist the homogenous by revealing beauty in what's already there. London is growing, and there are areas marked for change. There's now money to develop and regenerate them; with that comes a multitude of problems and fears. How are we implicated by working in that moment?

Ridley's rose and fell in less than a month, taking advantage of laws that allow for a 28 day temporary structure without a planning application

XAVI: If you don't have a market next door it just doesn't work. In other areas, it may be something different. I think the interesting thing about Ridley's was the system we put in place. Our whole practice and every project is a way of showing in a tangible way to others how you can take ownership of the places that you live in, how you can organize your site and look at interesting things without always waiting for someone above to say "yes" or "no" to something.

Now every brief that comes up from a council has one temporary project within it. So, it has been institutionalized, it has also been named as some sort of discipline. Our approach is more performative or involves events, but we're still part of that discipline that someone named "temporary architecture." Probably it would be more appropriate to call it "temporary acts."

CAROLINA: It is working constantly with this duality: making something for the community and, at the same time, balancing it by making something that the council will be happy to photograph and use to put the area on the map to sell it to developers. It is a real negotiation and a real sense of responsibility.

We do refer to our beginnings. Last year was five years since Ridley's and we used it as a moment of reflection. Sometimes my fear is making only things that are "beautiful" in the city, because public life and real life are a bit messy. There is a trend of doing things that are very beautiful to photograph, and by doing only this you are communicating a certain message and you're instantly excluding certain people.

I think the question becomes who we work with, because most of our work has been with local authorities. There are dangers with working with a developer, because your work can be used for "artwashing" – used to get great pictures or to make a community feel like something is being done for them, but in reality, there are much bigger processes happening in the background that will effectively shift and move everyone.

XAVI: Five years ago we would have said that we would never work with developers. But then, you slowly realise that the important thing is how you approach that task and how you make that relationship something that you think is positive and you consider the impact of your input. Sometimes it is more powerful to be inside than to be outside. What is interesting about the times that we're living in now is how activism is very productive. It is not all the time this voice from outside that moans and criticizes the system, but it is about finding ways to go inside. If we get ourselves inside a process with developers rather than being outside, at least we can try. But I think it is about how you position yourself as a practitioner, what context you are working in. Context is everything.

Diners sat at a communal table high above the market. Meals prepared in the ground floor kitchen were raised by a mechanical table up to the guests above

EVERYBODY'S HOUSE

THE ROSA PARKS HOUSE PROJECT

by RYAN & FABIA MENDOZA, JOÃO JOSÉ SANTOS, DIOGO VALE

The Rosa Parks House Project is the result of a series of interactions that began in Detroit, Michigan, where a decaying house on S. Deacon Street was placed on a list for demolition. The home of civil rights activist, Rosa Parks, from 1957-1959, it was saved from demolition in 2016 when her niece, Rhea McCauley, purchased it from the city of Detroit and gave it to artist, Ryan Mendoza. It catapulted out of obscurity due to the interventions of Mendoza, who moved the structure, or what was left of it, across the Atlantic Ocean to Berlin, Germany. There, it gained a new identity and notoriety through reconstruction on German soil. Transformed through this act of translocation, the structure would re-cross the ocean, with hopes of a repatriation through Brown University's sponsorship in spring of 2018.

At Int|AR, we rejoiced that this project - steeped in art, history, preservation, memory and, of course, adaptive reuse – would be in our own backyard. On a late February afternoon, we met the delivery of the shipping containers that crossed the Atlantic with the deconstructed parts of 2672 S. Deacon Street. These were unloaded at its temporary American home: WaterFire Arts Center in Providence, RI, a 37,000 sq ft arts venue that was itself transformed from an abandoned industrial facility for the US Rubber Company. The physical components of the humble structure occupied merely a corner of this vast interior, still marked with traces of its manufacturing past.

In the first days of March, the house slowly began to materialize from the bundles of house parts. We became acquainted with Ryan Mendoza and his team as they began to assemble the Providence rendition of 2672 S. Deacon Street with salvaged parts that comprised facades, partial wood flooring and elements of the internal staircase. Once a simple wood frame structure, the house's structural integrity was undermined

The side facade of 2672 S. Deacon Street in the process of reassembly at WaterFire Arts Center

From arrival to construction: the process of reassembly of the *Rosa Parks House Project* at the WaterFire Arts Center

by the deterioration of the second floor. In Berlin, this was resolved by augmenting the undermined structure with new framing. This permitted the presentation of the house as an object in Mendoza's Berlin garden. In Providence, where the house would also be presented as a whole object inside the exhibition hall of WaterFire Arts Center, team architects, João José Santos and Diogo Vale, designed a new glu-lam structural ring frame to provide additional support from the inside. But the construction was interrupted by the sudden withdrawal of support from Brown University for the project. The house was only a skeletal frame when the work came to an abrupt halt.

The ensuing March days were filled with speculations on the fate of the Rosa Parks House Project going forward. The barrage of media coverage of this controversial time is easily accessible and, therefore, not the subject of this article. A glance at the headlines would, however, reveal raw emotions, just under the surface, elicited by the return of this simple house to a country that had not come to terms with racism, half a century after the start of the Civil Rights movement. With an imminent deadline for the return of the house to Berlin, WaterFire Arts Center planned a public viewing of the project on the first weekend in April, heralding the 50-year anniversary of the assassination of Dr. Martin Luther King, Jr. Organized with scant time and resources, this celebration of the house was powered by good will and volunteerism. The haste to present the project without the previously promised funding placed enormous strain on the team as they attempted to complete the installation in a few days. In the end, the time constraints were insurmountable and the final product included only partially completed facades and roof.

These circumstances in Providence, however, yielded unprecedented views into the interior, a departure from its previous iterations. In Detroit, where the house was a ruin, the interior had succumbed to mold and rot. In Berlin, as an object in Mendoza's garden, curtains at the windows precluded a view of the non-existent interior. In Providence, where the house was unwittingly presented in an incomplete state, the interior – or lack thereof - was made visible for the first time, revealing Santos and Vale's intervention of a new internal structure. It also permitted views of two installations: first, the original second floor doors were suspended in the air where they would have been and, second, the inclusion of three ceramic sculptures by Mendoza, designed in consultation with Rhea McCauley. This incomplete state exposed the scantiness of the original material and, by contrast, emphasized the additions made to support the structure, all previously out of sight in Berlin. While applying conventional standards for heritage to the project may raise questions of authenticity and significance, in an era that includes "experimental preservation," this rendition of 2672 S. Deacon is one that opens a new chapter in the history of the house.

At Int|AR, we were drawn to the Rosa Parks House Project for its complexity. Once a humble wood home in Detroit, it became an "art object" when placed out of context and, repatriated, has claims as a monument of American civil rights – all through various acts of intervention. What indeed is the Rosa Parks House Project? How do we categorize it? Can we define it? What is the process by which it was transformed? What is its legacy and role in history? What constitutes a monument? Who has the right to assign values to monuments?

Few will have the opportunity to see this project in person and to probe these questions through observation. Herein, we provide the different perspectives on the project from its origins in Detroit to the journeys it has taken to date. We hope that by hearing the voices of not only Ryan Mendoza but that of the team behind the project's realization the reader will have an opportunity to claim 2672 S. Deacon Street for themselves. Rosa Parks' civil disobedience on that bus so long ago in Alabama was an act for a collective right, the house that provided her refuge for two years after Alabama and was saved from demolition is one that belongs to more than one person. It is Everybody's House.

—Liliane Wong, Int|AR

Ryan Mendoza reassembling the house in Berlin, Germany

*It began with **Ryan Mendoza**, American artist and expatriate living in Germany. In his own words:*

Before getting involved in the 2672 S. Deacon Street, *Rosa Parks House Project*, I was 25 years an expatriate living in Berlin. Having lost touch with my country, I thought, rather than distance myself further from American values, I would embrace them fully in attempt to epitomize the quintessential American by colonizing Europe with actual American houses. *The White House Project* began thanks to a house donated by a friend of mine, native Detroiter Gregg Johnson. The house was appropriately, though not without controversy, removed from Stoepel Street just off of Eight Mile, the road that divides a segregated Detroit.

Through *The White House Project* - where a house was deconstructed, shipped overseas and rebuilt at the Verbeke Foundation in Belgium - I gained adequate knowledge of how wooden houses could be disassembled and reassembled.

On my trips back and forth to Detroit I met, at a performance at the Charles H. Wright Museum, Gregg Dunmore and Joel Boykin of Pulsebeat.TV. After hearing of my desire to preserve American houses that would otherwise be demolished, they put me into contact with Rosa Parks' niece, Rhea McCauley.

I met Rhea on a wintry day in front of 2672 S. Deacon Street where the 3-bedroom house Rosa Parks had lived in with 15 family members stood in a decaying stoicism. I remember the floors were dipping and the house moved ever so slightly with the wind, the back wall being patched together with the doors of the house itself.

Both projects I had completed in Detroit, *The Invitation* and *The White House*, dealt with the housing crisis, a subtext that is also inextricable from the *Rosa Parks House Project*. Rhea McCauley, who had lived in the house with her aunt, had recently bought it off of a demolition list for 500 dollars. When local government and institutions showed no interest in helping her restore the house as a monument, she approached me and suggested we work together. Our petition for local support was also turned down, so I offered to ship the house to Berlin. It proved essential that the house be extricated from its location for the world to pay attention.

For lack of a more appropriate place, the unassuming house Rosa Parks had taken refuge in after the tumultuous Alabama bus boycott was temporarily relocated to the garden between my studio and my home in Berlin. Last winter, the house arrived to my doorstep as planks of wood in a shipping container and was rebuilt from sketches made during disassembly in Detroit. Reconstructing the house alone, and underfunded during the winter of 2016, was a physically challenging task. Handling the planks, I considered whether the house would one day become the 77th monument to the Civil Rights Movement. I read up on American history where

2672 S. Deacon displayed as an object inside the WaterFire Arts Center

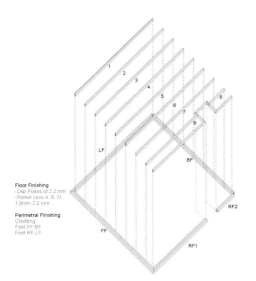

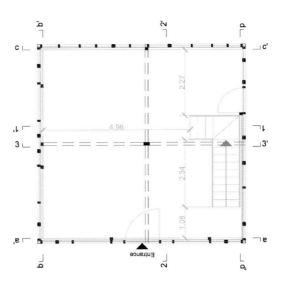

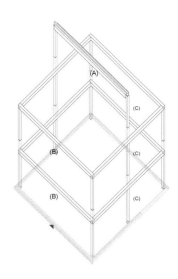

our forefathers were also slave owners and I struggled with this cognitive dissonance. Thomas Jefferson was undeniably a racist as well as a rather abusive slave-holder, notably punishing his slaves by selling them at auction, willfully breaking families apart. His only plausible solution to the problem of slavery included expatriation:

> "I can say with conscious truth that there is not a man on earth who would sacrifice more than I would, to relieve us from this heavy reproach ... if, in that way, a general emancipation and expatriation could be effected: ... but, as it is, we have the wolf by the ear, and we can neither hold him, nor safely let him go. Justice is in one scale, and self-preservation in the other."
> Letter from Thomas Jefferson to John Holmes, April 22, 1820 [1]

Jefferson worried the flesh would be ripped from the face of the nation, revealing an unsavory truth. Subsequent systematic transfer of enchainment, from slavery itself to segregation through the Jim Crow laws to a privatized prison system, kept the 'wolf' in chains, and the so-called preservation of the face of the nation intact. But with mounting evidence of systemic racism, and with clarity over what the confederate monuments actually stand for -having been created in a reactionary way to the advancements to civil equality- an opening for the Rosa Parks House to be preserved and possibly celebrated as a monument contrasts with its near demolition at the hands of the local government in Detroit.

During the reconstruction of the house, handling delicately the planks of wood, I wondered: was my mission that of preserving history or was it that of attempting to free the ever-ensnared Jeffersonian wolf, therefore upsetting a national myth? In the end, I realized I

am just custodian and messenger. The actual message, I myself, being born white and after the Civil Rights Movement, can only be comprehended in a limited way.

Rosa Parks came to Detroit fleeing death threats, but experienced little refuge in Detroit. After living for 2 years with her brother, sister-in-law and their 13 children, Parks moved multiple times. She suffered an assault in her home at the age of 81 and was threatened with eviction at 91. While Detroit was briefly renowned as a place where black residents reached significant levels of home ownership, Rosa Parks never owned a home. She called Detroit 'the Northern promise land that wasn't.' Housing issues, centered around segregation and displacement due to urban renewal, were central to Rosa Parks' activism her entire life. Detroit has ranked among the 10 most segregated metropolitan areas in the United States since the mid-20th century. By the early 1960s, urban renewal and highway construction destroyed 10,000 structures in Detroit, displacing over 40,000 people, 70% of whom were African-American. More recently, since the housing crisis, foreclosure and demolition swept the city, leaving more than 70,000 abandoned buildings and 90,000 vacant lots. [2]

For over 40 years, these four walls and roof were a home. It was the place that Rosa Parks' brother sought to create a better life for his family after returning from World War II, where Rosa Parks' nieces and nephews grew up and where Parks lived for her first two years in Detroit. When the family left in 1982, memories continued to cling to the clapboards, but the home became a house. When it was put on a demolition list in 2013, the meaning attached to the building changed again, it became a number on a list, a statistic in Detroit's decline. In its ensuing incarnations, the structure blurred lines between historic monument and art object.

Ultimately, this is a project about memory. By taking

Santos and Vale's diagrams for the new internal structure supporting the reassembled house

the house apart and then piecing it back together, literally 're-membering' it, Rhea McCauley and I invite the American consciousness to remember a house it didn't know it had forgotten. Art often plays with a shift in context to inspire the viewer to look: the house's stay in Berlin leveraged this discordance to get the viewer to pay attention. The house offers a unique opportunity to consider how we remember Rosa Parks, and in doing so, begins to renegotiate how we memorialize American history more broadly.

Recent debate surrounding the dismantling of confederate monuments indicates the persistent significance of how we inscribe memories into the topography of our surroundings. 700 monuments of Robert E. Lee and other Confederate generals still parade across public squares and school grounds across the United States, despite a recent wave of dismantling. Confederate monuments rely on erasing the context of their construction to foster nostalgia. Confederate monument construction peaked in 1910, a year after the NAACP was founded. Another flurry of building began in the 1950s as the Civil Rights Movement gained momentum. The Little Rock Nine and school integration prompted a disturbing spike of Confederate monuments on school campuses. Many Americans are under the illusion, however, that the monuments were built during reconstruction. The anachronistic material and design veil the racism that is inextricable from these totems.

I highlight this disconnect in context in order to introduce the way the *Rosa Parks House Project* can offer a mode of memorialization, where context is paramount. Of course, the version of Rosa Parks incorporated into the American mythos has also relied on obscured context and idealized narrative. In her biography, *The Rebellious Life of Mrs. Rosa Parks*, Jeanne Theoharis exposes the ways in which the historical narrative surrounding Rosa Parks has reduced her lifelong commitment to activism to one afternoon on a bus, fabricated a story of a quiet seamstress who demurely kept her seat and relegated Parks to be a hero for children. In the introduction of her book, Theoharis emphasizes, "One of the greatest distortions of the Parks fable has been the ways it made her meek.... When Parks died in Detroit in 2005, she was held up as a national heroine but stripped of her lifelong history of activism and anger at American injustice. The Parks who emerged was a self-sacrificing mother figure for a nation who would use her death for a ritual of national redemption." Parks' memorial services also took place in the wake of Hurricane Katrina. In honoring Rosa Parks, the nation was able to glaze over the racial and economic inequality exposed by government negligence during Katrina. The public memorial leveraged a romantic fable of Rosa Parks to quiet, contemporary injustice.

My hope is that, by contrast, the dissonant context at play in the *Rosa Parks House Project* will impede nostalgia and obstruct simplification. The house's journey across the sea should inspire questions. Addressing history and the present day with questions, rather than assumptions or generalizations, is a mode of demanding a fuller version of history.

Ryan Mendoza

*Team member **Fabia Mendoza**'s film on the project, The White House Documentary, received an award at the 18th Beverly Hills Festival in April 2018. She lends her voice to this article with thoughts that provide a cinematic background to the house's place of origin:*

Ryan started his first project, *The White House,* with the intention to reconnect with his home country. It was meant as a project about memory. It was serendipity that our friend, Gregg Johnson, who wanted to donate

Santos and Vale's catalog of parts and their proposal for support
elements allowed the house to be reassembled after its relocation
from Berlin, Germany

the house for this project, happened to be a Detroiter.

Without the plan to make a political project or one about the Civil Rights Movement, Ryan walked into a battlefield of racial tensions, controversy, political rot and, 3 years later, came back to Germany with the Rosa Park's Family Home donated to him by Rosa Parks' family.

Ryan became the embodiment of The White Savior Complex. And the unsuccessful attempt by Rosa Parks' family members to save the structure and the fact that Ryan was able to do so became proof of a system in which black oral history is not valued.

The White House Documentary, 75min, 2017 began as a simple documentary about an artist, but the habitants, musicians and friends we collaborated with on the various projects in the city took more and more space in my movie.

I hoped to portray Detroit as a place that can't be reduced to its ruins.

As in fact it is a melting pot of musical talent and wisdom. Living through segregation, the rebellions in 1967, the housing crisis and the downfall of the automobile industry, the Detroiters who resisted the City's depopulation were left with a deep fighting spirit and untouchable pride.

313- One Love, Detroit vs. Everybody, Nothing Stops Detroit tell the story of a city, unwilling to surrender.

The image portrayed of Detroit as an abandoned city couldn't be farther from the truth.

I learned how the Detroit Techno by Underground Resistance, exported to Berlin in the 90ies, shaped my own city and made it the metropolis it is today.

Experiencing the gentrification of Detroit's downtown area, the progress of projects like the Packard Plant Project on Detroit's East side, the biggest industrial renovation project in North America, the Berlin-Detroit Connection, a cultural program between the both cities, and the new train system are all evidence of Detroit's comeback. I can only hope that city planning and gentrification are being guided correctly in order to positively influence all communities.

Fabia Mendoza

2672 S. Deacon reassembled in the artist's garden in Berlin, Germany

Closeup and through the clapboard to the interior
of the *Rosa Parks House Project*

2672 S. Deacon on the demolition list in Detroit, Michigan

Architect Diogo Vale, team member for disassembling and reassembling the house both in Berlin and in Providence posits this project by looking backward in history:

It becomes interesting when one thinks about the power that architecture can physically transmit to society; going back from the opulent and luxurious buildings in the Baroque era to the political and monumental buildings of the Neoclassical period. The weight of authority - as meaning, as modus operandi – is transmitted through the scale and detail of such buildings all over the world.

In the XXI century, in a bankrupt city, the historical heritage of the local community starts to lose meaning for its government and they began to demolish traces of a built history deeply rooted to the city. With this simple house on the verge of being forgotten (demolished) begins a polemic among the community. In a way, its significance increases with no change in scale or detail. In that sense, it is beautiful that a simple word "Unforgotten" unleashes a sequence of socio-political events....

A simple and worn out house with no architectural signature becomes a curious tool for creating an environment for a debate on different subjects but all with the same goal: an improvement of the quality of life.

The past is revisited as a learning tool to create knowledge, to discuss the future, to move forward, to delete taboos and all because of a simple architectonic maneuver. Detached from the surroundings, the house emanates a different message, on the loss of a country that didn't appreciate the value of its simple but historic monumentality.

And from the strength of one person more layers are added, more people become involved, increasing the value and meaning of this house. Its return to its home country is a perfect moment - to discuss, debate about the society and community it has formed.

From a simple worn out family house to the house for everybody. Once again architecture serves as messenger of a group of important values, but by the hand of an artist and a house that knows no luxury. Neither palace or political building this humble little structure holds the same power to transmit messages and inform its people. Rosa Parks House, the house of everybody!

Diogo Vale

Architect João José Santos, co-producer of the new internal support structure, instead shares his thoughts on the role of supporting Ryan Mendoza and what it means to add a new layer to history.

House...as Home, will always be an undisputed symbol of our continuously developing human identity, as we move on and from. As a real-life American hero story, this house of many is then a singular subject, for it had not only been the place of heartful familial gathering but

the intimate shelter found later in the storm. Witness of circumstances, moulded by them, informs who inhabits it and how it is inhabited, representing at the same time millions in a collective identity. Today the quiet structure of statements from the past still stands and, an inside-out room for collective consideration, it is again formed, readapted, just like Home.

Rosa Louise McCauley Parks, as home for American historic memory and national identity.

There were three main acts to consider for an assembly/disassembly process of this project since it landed in Wedding, Berlin, in 2016; to dissect the one-man job, to re-formulate it, to recreate it.

To dissect

To learn from the artist and his work as pre-conditions. Acknowledge problems and solutions found upon giving literal and physical shape to this idea, reckoning with little or no assistance from anybody else. Recognize the small assisting construction features created for this purpose and know the new structural system cast in order to make possible this solo "free-style reconstruction."

To re-formulate

To sum up professional knowledge of the already formed construction for making it a safe, transferable object. Collaborating with both engineering and architectural disciplines as past crutches and innocuous parts are removed, a new sub-structural system is designed and an inventory of the parts and the assembly catalogue are made, all aiming for a final result.

To recreate

To rescue a kidnapped house when the project finds a 'lasting' new home, when the figure arises from an embodiment of the artist and the personal approach by the building assisting team that, in a collective work, will positively leave new imprints. In a communal accomplishment, the work of art slowly drops authorship to become everybody's work, everybody's house.

João José Santos

EPILOGUE
At the date of printing, the *Rosa Parks House Project* has once again been disassembled. Its future is unknown as it will be put up for auction.

ENDNOTES:

1 Letter of Thomas Jefferson to John Holmes, Library of Congress https://www.loc.gov/exhibits/jefferson/ 159.html, accessed June 26, 2018

2 https://www.liveauctioneers.com/item/63230011_the-rosa-parks-family-home, accessed July 2, 2018

The *Rosa Parks House Project* on exhibit at the WaterFire Arts Center

Play Lancaster is a project of Public Workshop that teaches local youth design-build skills and gathers community volunteers to construct street-front play space on a struggling commercial corridor

(photo@Public Workshop)

TACTICAL URBANISM WHERE IT MATTERS

SMALL SCALE INTERVENTIONS IN UNDERSERVED COMMUNITIES

by SALLY HARRISON

Tactical Urbanism and the Creative Class

In 2005 a collaborative of artists and designers paid for two hours at a parking meter and installed turf, chairs and a potted tree. Inspired by stealth interventions of artists like Banksey and the Situationists, the parking space installation by the San Francisco group Rebar posed a critique of cultural values embedded in the use of urban space. [1] The idea of natural and human elements invading a space designated for car storage, and visitors finding a pleasurable respite in a parking space, became iconic. Images went viral.

Two years later, this spatial détournement had become an international event: Park(ing) Day became an opportunity for young designers to express their creativity and assert the right to claim public space, if only for an afternoon. Rebar's instant global success is often cited as the beginning of the movement now called "tactical urbanism." [2] Employing small-scale, short term interventions to return vibrancy to city life and "seed structural environmental change," tactical urbanism tapped into the estrangement of the common citizen from having a role in shaping cities. [3] Though various iterations have retained a seriousness of intent with a view to addressing critical, environmental and

social issues, the once subversive Park(ing) Day is now an annual staple of celebratory, "fun urban design." As the leading edge of the tactical urbanist movement, Park(ing) Day has engendered a cascade of novel, engaging interventions made and enjoyed by members of the young creative class. Pop-up markets and beer gardens, chair-bombing, hand-made wayfinding tactics, downtown beaches and unsanctioned bike-lanes are hallmarks of casual-chic tactical urbanism in cities worldwide - a brand itself.

Begun as spontaneous, community-generated activism, tactical urbanism - with the tag line "lighter, quicker, cheaper," or "LQC" in the parlance of the Project for Public Places - has been popularized in various media and exhibited in prestigious venues, guaranteeing mainstream acceptance. [4] Almost as quickly, tactical urbanism has attracted city leaders and the development community seeking opportunities to promote gentrifying neighborhoods with an allure of hipness. Installations become nothing more than a marketing tool, stealthily reversing the grass roots ethos of the movement. [5] A favorite of young urbanites is the much replicated pop-up-beer-garden-in-vacant-lot. Vaguely reminiscent of a suburban backyard barbecue with its picnic tables, kegs and Adirondack chairs, the beer garden tactic has been seized by the development community to promote so-called "emerging" neighborhoods by creating a familiar, nonthreatening scene – a strategy for attracting young, white gentrifiers into poor strategically located neighborhoods where they might otherwise feel uncomfortable living, and for the unwitting neighbors a kind of pacification through lot clean-up. [6] Sadly, these techniques have been remarkably successful.

Informality and Urban Space

Urban tactics have been around as long as there have been cities: the street vendor, the sidewalk lounger, the child at play, the graffiti artist, the squatter, the guerrilla gardener – all have taken their corner of the city and appropriated it for individual or collective use. [7] Historically urban tactics have been open to all. Those without privilege survive through creative inventions, and have utilized the city opportunistically: finding unclaimed space, using available materials, bending the rules to accommodate needs unmet by the powerful entities that plan and organize their environment. Without self-celebration these urban tacticians operate in what de Certeau calls the drifts and ellipses of the urban order – by-passing or overwriting with lived experience the formal strategies of the top-down city. [8]

Designed and built by PhilaNOMA (Philadelphia Chapter of the National Organization of Minority Architects), this seasonal installation extends the library's literacy mission into the neighborhood
(photo@PhilaNOMA)

While tactical urbanism has deep roots in age-old informal practices of urban dwellers, its contemporary iteration can be traced to mid-century resistance against modernist planning and bureaucracy – articulated at length by Lefebvre, Rudofsky, Alexander, Jacobs, Team Ten and others. Van Eyck of Team Ten decried postwar redevelopment as "mile upon mile of organized nowhere, and nobody feeling he is 'somebody living somewhere.' No microbes left –yet each citizen a disinfected pawn on a chessboard, but no chessmen -- hence no challenge, no duel no dialogue. ... Architects have left no cracks and crevices this time. They expelled all sense of place. Fearful as they are of the wrong occasion, the unpremeditated event, the spontaneous act...." [9]

The call to human-centered design provoked study of everyday spatial practices. These were undertaken in non-western contexts such as Rudolfsky's 1964-65 ground-breaking exhibition at MoMA and subsequent book, *Architecture Without Architects*, but also in the epicenter of corporate power, by William Whyte in his famous New York City plaza studies. Partly due to his accessible language and non-threatening tone, and partly to the rigor of his observational methods, Whyte's contributions have helped to popularize an understanding of urban dynamics. His observations astutely (though often hilariously dated) point out simple truths about informal, spontaneous use of highly formal space: access to food, moveable seating and "triangulation." It is not surprising that Whyte has become the godfather of the current tactical urbanism/placemaking movement. [10]

Though Whyte's work is important, it is apolitical. He opens his film "The Social Life of Small Urban Spaces" with scenes of street life in Harlem (circa 1969), but it is a sentimental depiction of otherness, with "no challenge, no duel" that would address the larger inequities of urban space.

Tactical Urbanism for Whom? Stories from Two Sides of the Same River [11]
Tactical urbanism and placemaking projects have chiefly concerned themselves with activating underutilized space in almost-healthy, well-served environments. [12] Indeed, prerequisite conditions are cited in the *Project for Public Spaces* website: "Once components like accessibility, safety, and overall comfort have been addressed, it may be the right moment to think about some LQC strategies." [13] That excess of caution certainly contradicts the movement's stated desire to seed structural environmental change; it precludes those places that may most urgently need well-designed catalytic interventions - in underserved urban neighborhoods accessibility, safety and overall comfort are among the chief issues that undermine active social spaces that build community. Add to this high household poverty levels and inadequate public funding and the result

is that lighter, quicker and cheaper is most often the only option. In view of this, a discussion about a new iteration of tactical urbanism in places where it really matters is important and timely.

Despite being known for its recovery from post-industrial depopulation through the ascendancy of its creative class, Philadelphia has another narrative. Its twenty-six percent poverty rate exceeds that of the ten largest cities in the US, and directly across the river Camden, New Jersey is the poorest city in the country. Citizens of both Philadelphia and Camden suffer deep unemployment, a predominance of single-parent households with high numbers of children, low educational attainment and poor health. Consistently, residents report the isolating impact of drug culture and criminal activity and the erosive effects that the concentration of vacant lots have in their neighborhoods. [14] These are not conditions in which small, temporary acts of design intervention can easily ignite significant change. Nevertheless design centered in a deep understanding of place provides a more hopeful perspective. Even - and especially - in these most profoundly underserved neighborhoods there are patterns of citizen action that are creative and pragmatic spatial responses both to need and to opportunity; here as in impoverished neighborhoods around the world, in Cathy Lang Ho's words, "what we call tactical urbanism is simply a way of life." [15] Designers with a commitment to broader social impact might find ways to collaborate with communities who know their own landscape, and together develop urban tactics to tap veins of unrealized possibility.

How can a new version of tactical urbanism be employed to advance a social justice agenda and reclaim democratizing effects of the movement? How, outside the centers and contested gentrifying periphery, can small scale design-interventions address the multi-layered quality-of-life issues born of poverty and public underinvestment? What must be added to the "spontaneous" act of intervention to make sure that it knowingly engages larger spatial, socio-economic and temporal contexts? Who participates, and how do designers, who are mostly outsiders, operate?

Play, Tactics in the Interstices
On Lancaster Avenue, a struggling commercial corridor in West Philadelphia, play is a vehicle for social and physical health. Play Lancaster, led by the design collaborative Public Workshop, teaches youth within the local neighborhood skills in building and designing urban space. Eschewing the guerilla-designer as Robin Hood role, Public Workshop draws enthusiasts and skeptics alike into a collective ethos of placemaking. The group has an established collaborative history with the local CDC that has been at work on revitalization strategies for the Avenue, and Public Workshop

has demonstrated long term commitment to the neighborhood and evolution of the project by co-inhabiting a storefront near the play site.

The neighborhood-generated idea for Play Lancaster began with an empty lot that called out to be a playground. However, the 80' by 100' lot on the Avenue defied the security principles of natural surveillance: no surprise that it was soon revealed as a nighttime drug hangout. Undeterred, Public Workshop and its young crew first enclosed the deep back of the lot with a decorative fence and lockable gate, reducing the play area to a ten-foot band along the Avenue. Not exactly expelling the intermittent drug users, the enclosed off-street space was gradually colonized by youth activities, becoming a seasonal workshop for future community design-build projects.

The street-front play scape is owned by the neighborhood. Fun and informal, this strip merges with the public space of Lancaster Avenue. Public Workshop furnished it with a community chalk board, a platform with table for eating and relaxing, a "switchback play bench," a mini-fort and simple exercise equipment. Counter to the traditional design of playgrounds as unique bounded areas, the play space spills out on to the street for hopscotch and other pavement games. It operates in the spirit of Christopher Alexander's observation, "Play takes place in the interstices of adult life. As they play children become full of their surroundings…"[16] Indeed, the sidewalk is where city kids, instinctive tacticians, have always played - out in the carnival of street life, but also under the watchful eye of parents and neighbors.

Understanding the ecosystem of the neighborhood, Public Workshop saw the potential for this tactical intervention to both thrive and to have a critical impact at a larger scale. Despite the lot's reputation as a tough corner, it is directly adjacent to a popular deli, across the street are a daycare and after school center, and around the corner a charter school, all filled with kids who gravitate to the site.

The founder of Public Workshop says he wants to "rewire the community engagement process" by making it tangible, visible and animated by the creative energy of youth. While at work on Lancaster Avenue, the crew drew wide participation from diverse members of the community: some helped build, some set up chessboards, some gave advice. Some were part of the very drug culture whose space the project had appropriated, but as is common, many were related to participants and became invaluable as guardians of the site. [17]

Test Before You Invest: Reimagining the Public Realm in Camden

Nowhere are the challenges to the public realm as

Street games are age-old urban tactics. Children engage and re-create the world on their own terms but "in the interstices of the adult world"
(photo@Public Workshop)

evident as Camden, New Jersey, the poorest city in the country. Directly across the Delaware River from Philadelphia, Camden claims distinction as an active port city as well the home of an important university and hospital, but these assets cannot compensate for the depth of its poverty. The crisis of identity, of truly belonging neither to Philadelphia nor New Jersey, is painfully clear in its active recreational waterfront whose public spaces and amenities unapologetically turn their backs on the city. By contrast, in the experimental interventions within Roosevelt Plaza Park at the heart of Camden, democratic access to public space is the driver. The two-acre park replaced a demolished parking garage, but was only a windswept walk-through with few amenities that could build community and civic identity. Led by a public-private partnership and designed by landscape architects and planners Sikora Wells Appel and Group Melvin Design, the seasonal installation is ambitious and innovative in terms of design, program and research. Its tactics serve the placemaking principle of "test before you invest" famously used in the Times Square project, but now in a very different in context: Roosevelt Plaza Park is bordered by City Hall, a large methadone clinic, a Rutgers academic building and small scale commercial uses. [18]

Over three years of iterative placemaking – designing, building, studying, revising– the designers have been able to experiment freely with low-cost high-impact interventions, and observe how they engage the public. Sourced from the nearby port, Intermediate Bulk Containers (IBCs) are stacked to form towers as the centerpiece of the plaza where jazz concerts and other public events are held. Off to the side is the Grove, a node with moveable tables and chairs and brightly colored umbrellas interspersed with plantings. It serves as the "social room" of the site where the exceptionally diverse population in the area comes to lunch and hangs out with friends – city workers, out-patients from the methadone clinic, Rutgers students, neighborhood children. Here the social-bonding agent is a simple upright piano where people from every walk of life love to perform. This small but compelling intervention creates what William Whyte has famously called "triangulation," an urban event stimulating complete strangers to interact as if they know one another. [19]

The park is a work in progress. During the first year the IBC towers supported canopies, and the towers were lit from within to create a nighttime spectacle. Motion sensors changed the light color from cool to warm as people passed. In the second year the same cubes were reinstalled as vertical planters topped with rainwater-capturing saucers. These green towers and a rain curtain set the stage for a lively, interactive teaching demonstration about the water-based environmental problems facing Camden. And in the third year the green towers were reinstalled and concerts expanded; health

was introduced as a theme, with new food stands, play space, and exercise programming.

During each six-month installation the park was documented using time-lapse photography, video interviews, ground observations and postcard surveys. This documentation identified and mapped how the park was used and by whom, what worked and did not - methods straight from William Whyte. New ideas surfaced – more music events, more family-centered space, a playground, food carts, and, interestingly, an often-voiced concern over the excessive presence of "police" (potentially the uniformed park "ambassadors").[20] An overwhelming sense of satisfaction and pride infuses feedback from visitors. Says one: "Camden has been neglected for so long...and to have somebody just care enough to give this – it's the smallest thing but the biggest thing".[21] This is a poignant remark, at once validating the project's success and revealing a flaw. Perhaps the intensity of surveillance for research and safety has had the unintended consequence of distancing placemaking from the users. For all its generosity and focus on activity, the park is "given," rather than co-created with this hugely underserved community.

Night guardians. With broad support and engagement of the community, the playground is informally protected by older siblings of the primary users (photo@Public Workshop)

The interviewee's gratitude shimmers with awareness of endemic powerlessness, a recognition that others choose the agenda to serve the interests of the populace.

Rules of Engagement: Context, Commitment, and Collaboration

These very different cases speak to a how tactical urbanism might be used to advance social justice goals in underserved communities. However well-meant or cleverly conceived, designer-generated tactical urbanism applied in struggling neighborhoods is challenging; we cannot simply draw on the now-predictable social-space tropes to transform quality of life. While the ethic of unfettered pro-active intervention tempts designers to decide what is in the interest of the common good, in order to carry social impact, a design intervention – even one quite small – should evolve from a deep recognition of how the neighborhood works.

Thoughtful designers do have much to offer. Trained as we are in multi-scale research, representation, and making, we can help a community to create

Light towers. The stacked IBC cubes from local shipyard are the building blocks of the site, their verticality organizing the large open plaza. Lit from within they provide changing ambience at night
(photo@ Sikora Wells appel/Group Melvin Design)

a simultaneous reading of larger systems and locally practiced tactics, suggesting how and where intervention would be most effective. We understand that the tactical project itself cannot be a no-risk proposition. However much it may be lighter, quicker and cheaper, it is a commitment of some significance. It must be well-designed because what is temporary often becomes permanent.

A commitment to continued involvement further distinguishes these cases from the typical tactical urbanism project. Whereas in healthy environments, simply "seeding" might reasonably yield new and sustainable growth, in underserved communities the rough terrain presents significant obstacles to survival and continuity. At Roosevelt Park, it has taken years of vigorous programming, evaluation, redesign and reprogramming for patterns of human-centered civic expression to take root. Notwithstanding the disconcerting excess of oversight, the annual experiments in placemaking in this once bereft plaza have succeeded. And though the "LQC" tactics employed by the designers were meant to minimize risk for future capital expense, it may be that the vibrancy of change is the most valuable contribution to the long-term identity of the place.

Play Lancaster has also undergone constant change since its inception. Less about a fully-formed future vision than about a process that takes full advantage of trial and error, it has become a space that learns and teaches. Intentionally educative, the program challenges its young builders to balance the discipline of making with the porosity of creative thought. Inviting collaboration from all corners of the neighborhood, it also challenges the community to commit to its children. The seeming paradox of play, front and center in the public realm, literally spilling out on the sidewalk of a shopping corridor, tells us something important about what our society should value. Is this not what tactical urbanism is meant to do?

ENDNOTES:

1 Blaine Merker, "Taking Place: Rebar's absurd tactics in generous urbanism," in *Insurgent Public Space: Guerrilla Urbanism and the Remaking of Contemporary Cities*, ed. Jeffrey Hou (New York: Routledge, 2010): 42-51.

2 Mike Lydon and Anthony Garcia, *Tactical Urbanism 2: Short Term Action, Long Term Change*. (Washington: Island Press, 2012), and Susan Silberberg, "Places in the Making, how placemaking builds places and Communities", https://dusp.mit.edu/sites/dusp.mit.edu/files/attachments/project/mit-dusp-places-in-the-making.pdf. MIT Department of Urban Studies and Planning, Accessed May 12, 2016.

3 Merker, 49.

4 Three high-profile exhibits were mounted between 2008 and 2013: *Actions: What You Can Do With the City* (Canadian Center for Architecture); *Uneven Growth: Tactical Urbanisms for Expanding Megacities* (Museum of Modern Art) and *Spontaneous Interventions: design actions for the common good* (American Pavilion at the Venice Architecture Biennale).

5 Oli Mould, "Tactical Urbanism: The New Vernacular of the Creative City," *Geography Compass 8.8* (2014): 529–539.

See also: Gordon Douglas, "The formalities of informal improvement: technical and scholarly knowledge at work in do-it-yourself urban design," *Journal of Urbanism: International Research on Placemaking and Urban Sustainability* (2015): 1-18.

Gordon Douglas, "Do-it-yourself Urban Design in the Help Yourself City," in *Architecture Magazine: Spontaneous Interventions*, (August, 2012): 44.

6 Damon C. Williams, "Gentrification dispute revived," *Philadelphia Tribune*, February 20, 2016, http://www.phillytrib.com/news/gentrification-dispute-revived/article_e3d6f076-6878-5e92-9cb5-d3d94a3cfa8b.html. Accessed 3 June 2016.

7 See: John Chase, et al., *Everyday Urbanism*, (New York: Monacelli Press, 1999), and Ananya Roy and Nezzar AlSayyad, *Urban Informality: Transnation Perspectives from the Middle East, Latin America and South Asia*, (Oxford: Latham Press, 2004).

8 Michel de Certeau, "Spatial Practices: Walking in the City," in *Michel de Certeau*, trans. Steven F. Rendell (Berkeley: University of California Press, 1988), 91-110.

9 Aldo Van Eyck, "The Role of the Architect," in *Team 10 Primer*, ed. Alison Smithson, (Cambridge, MA: MIT Press, 1968), 44.

10 William Whyte, *The Social Life of Small Urban Spaces*, (New York: The Conservation Foundation, 1980). I use placemaking and tactical urbanism as co-related terms that both refer to iterative processes that support human centered use of public space. Generally, the spatial tactic is a (smaller) tool for (larger) placemaking.

11 Portions of the case studies of "Play Lancaster" and Roosevelt Plaza Park have been published in my article "Innovation: Tactical Urbanism in Underserved Communities," in *Context, the Journal of AIA Philadelphia* (Spring 2016).

12 Notable exceptions are Corona Plaza in Queens, NY; the Detroit Alleys Project; the Rebuild Foundation in St. Louis, the Village of Arts and Humanities in Philadelphia.

13 "The Lighter, Cheaper, Quicker Transformation of Public Spaces," *Project for Public Places*, http://www.pps.org/reference/lighter-quicker-cheaper/ Accessed 2 June, 2016.

14 Nila Luiz et al., "Quality of Life Plan", unpublished report by Asociacion Peurtorriquenos en Marcha, 2010.

15 Cathy Ho, "Spontaneous Interventions: Design Actions for the Common Good," in *Architecture Magazine: Spontaneous Interventions*, (August, 2012): 24.

16 Christopher Alexander, "A City is not a Tree," in *Architectural Design*, 206 (1966): 12.

17 Alex Giliam, Personal interview, January 22, 2016.

18 Lydon and Garcia, 36.

19 Whyte, 94-101.

20 Joseph Sikora, Personal Interview, Feb. 3, 2016.

21 Sikora Wells Appel and Melvin Group Design, Unpublished report, "Activating Roosevelt Plaza Park, Placemaking in Camden's Public Spaces," 2015.

WE ARE NEVER NOT INSIDE

DISCRETE OBJECTS AND NESTED INTERIORITIES

by CLAY ODOM

Hierarchies of resistance, manifest in the form of borders, border walls, envelopes, enclosures, and edges, are central to design and cultural discourse today. Certainly in the West, the practice of Architecture, and subsequently that of Interior Design, has been organized by the consideration and development of borders defined, for example, as rigid containments, separations, and delimitations of spaces by program.[1] In addition, traditional codified systems (including laws, building codes, rules, norms, pedagogies, theories and stylistic movements) often reinforce rigidity and resistance in design practices and associated engineering and building trades. Not surprisingly, these practices and codes also actively conspire in perpetuating, or even generating, a-priori hierarchical understandings of boundaries which rigidly divide environments, objects, and interiorities.

Digging deeper into this observation of both design paradigms and objective realities, we find that borders seem to prioritize oppositions such as inside v. outside or object v. space as well as dualities and hierarchy of material and form associated with demarcation of such interiority and exteriority. They resist effective interactions of objects and more complex systems of objects while also blocking much of their critical reconsideration. In its resistance, the clarity of opposition is black and white and creates a hierarchical world-view where objects people create are not 'in' but 'on' the world.[2] In addition, oppositional notions such as mind/body, us/them, public/private, natural/artificial, or nature/human, to name a few, have developed out of western classical thought; in fact, this type of separation is visualized, for example, in the 18th century maps created by Giambattista Nolli of that most classical of cities,

Rome.[3] The "Nollimaps" and later examples in Gestalt studies prioritize oppositional relationships of figure/ground or object/ space, and (even when 'reversed') we then see them as distinct and hierarchical (one above or greater than the other).

Further, these types of oppositions seem to reinforce anthropomorphic, or human-centric, actions and the negative environmental effects of the Anthropocene.[4] Foregrounding human actions in ways that are distinct and separated from an interior rather than linked to it, people operate independently of effect and therefore without consequence of individual actions which aggregate into larger systems. However, this separation may be overcome by reframing our work in relation to interiority rather than distinction from it. "This, then, is the paradox of the Anthropocene: the point at which we recognize our species to be a geologic force requires, simultaneously, the rejection of our metaphysical separation from nature."[5] Perhaps then entertaining a different view of these relations may be a beginning for recalibrating actions of design and theory today.

Today emerging theoretical frameworks and projects are beginning to re-situate relations between objects and spaces (including people), or better yet between forms of objects and spaces, both in and around the constructions. These contemporary works develop relations through objects and interiors which both aggregate and interact in localized and non-hierarchical ways. These works reframe how we understand and operate in the world and serve as alternatives to existing modernist dogma which prioritizes gestalt, figure-ground forms of hierarchy. Contemporary examples include theories such as Object Oriented Ontology and Post-Humanism, meaning 'beyond humanism', which seek to re-situate

RC8_Scendobia_Perspective_NewYork
(photo@ Daniel Koehler)

the relationships between people, objects, relations, and effects.[6] These previously hierarchical relationships, seen typically in order from people to objects to space and environment, may be understood in a more nuanced spectrum. This new domain is situated between the explicit or externalized and the 'withdrawn.'[7]

Reconsidering duality by engaging with contemporary theories outlined above, ranging from Post-Humanism and Object Oriented Ontology to engaging issues of Phenomenology and Atmospheres, we might come to a vital new understanding. In short, we begin to realize that everything, from buildings and parks to people and planets, can be understood as objects and effects.[8] By extension, "we are coming to realize that human places exist within and alongside thousands and thousands of nonhuman places, overlapping, intersecting, and interpenetrating with 'our' place."[9] Objects, which now include people, spaces, and effects, as well as physical constructs, are multi-scaled, layered, nested, overlapped, containing, and contained by other objects and object-like interiorities. In our daily life we find examples of this through experience. For example, we may understand that as we move out of objects such as buildings, we move into other objects that we call public spaces. To follow, we may understand that, as we move out of cities, we move into suburbs. If we continue this trajectory, we not only expand in scale, but we also see that we are always moving through, across, or between borders 'into' another interior. We may then come to realize that perhaps we aren't ever fully outside.[10] Further, we might even begin to consider that our day-to-day experiences are of interiors of objects, and we are never not inside them.[11]

What are explicit examples interior designers and architects might reference when they interrogate, activate, and synthesize object-oriented interior relationships between larger and smaller objects? Returning to the framework of varied, layered relations as suggested in the illustrations, architect and professor Tom Wiscombe creates a compelling pair of analogies. He writes that, "a sack gathers things together into a loosely coherent form without dissolving the things' discreteness...this theory suggests multiple outsides and insides, and an infinite deferral of interiority, like drilling sideways through a set of Russian dolls...buildings become objects, wrapped in objects, wrapped in object and so on." As either sack of objects or nested objects, borders in these powerful analogies become the defining points of articulation between interiorities. Most likely, these borders exhibit different tendencies for formal or spatial readings depending on which side relations of people and/or objects occur. Although the readings of nested interiorities in these examples are subjectively contingent, the relationships are autonomous. Therefore in order to break a tendency to dualism, objects (existing either within interiorities of larger objects, or enclosing smaller objects) should be understood and developed to articulate and promote a range of interactions-with and autonomy-from their human and non-human neighbors.[12]

When challenging hierarchy and rigidity, we might be tempted to reinforce existing paradigms of digital form and space which prioritize unification, gradation, or smoothness as actionable concepts and operations. This type of smoothness is one characteristic of early digital projects. This is perhaps most evident in continuous gradation and curvatures, facilitated by software operations such as 'lofting'. This is also developed within the 'blob' projects from the 1990s and early 2000s by architects such as Greg Lynn, and outlined in his seminal exhibition "Intricacy."[13] More recently this is a characteristic of what is called parametric 'style,' espoused most famously by Patrik Schumacher.[14] 'Parametricism' in this case describes formal, spatial, and stylistic outcomes of continuous transformations between conditions, rather than articulating explicit and localized, or discrete, difference. Critically, however, this simply masks oppositional thinking as critical design operation while ignoring the question of articulation.

These theories are also being addressed in speculative practices which explore the development of local conditions and relations which are articulated locally, and perhaps roughly, rather than concealed within either smooth continuities or hierarchical part-whole concepts. Today, these types of relations, articulated between objects, are being characterized as 'discrete.'

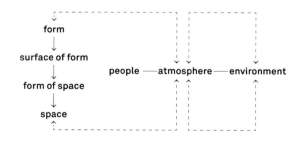

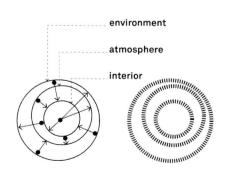

LEFT
Diagram escribing nesting objects of interiority
atmosphere and environment
RIGHT
Diagram expanding the relationship of nested interiority and points for possible articulation
between interiors, objects, people, and environments

Historian Mario Carpo traces the rise of the discrete in relation to contemporary practices where the idea has developed through digital tools and assembly-based material computation. In his essay 'Excessive Resolution,' Carpo writes 'discreteness is...now embedded in most software," following with how material forms of computation are being developed which capture "the inherent discreteness of nature."[15] The projects and frameworks emerging from these practices critically reconsider ideas of anthropocentrism, hierarchy, and duality while defining new modes for theory and design based on objects, interiors, and their active articulation.

Today, through theories of object-orientation and discreteness, objects and interactions are being reconsidered not as smooth continuities but rather as localized conditions articulated within even larger sets of objects and situations. Describing a quality of irregularity informed by discreteness, Timothy Morton has written "from the standpoint of the genuinely postmodern ecological era, what has collapsed is (the fantasy of empty, smooth) space....The world is so much more independent of us and so much more playful than that."[16] The independence of discrete objects (as physical and spatial formations as well as systemic conditions) allows multiple forms of 'playful' relationship and articulation to occur.

Ultimately, "if everything is a whole object and not a part of something else, and everything exists equally but differently, then vertical stratification between parts and wholes becomes impossible...everything exists side by side."[17] Laterally reframing and dismantling traditional hierarchies therefore becomes a tool used to reconsider architecture and interior design in the Anthropocene. Human-made or not, in this view, objects' interactions are varied and non-hierarchical. They may generate or affect smaller and larger conditions while also maintaining ontological and situational 'differences' as varying degrees of autonomy depending on the interactions.[18]

In order to test the theoretical frameworks described above, we must expand our understanding of discrete relations within design itself. Returning to Mario Carpo,

who has tracked the "turn" from smoothness toward the discrete in contemporary digital design and fabrication, we understand articulation through "the inherent discreteness of nature (which, after all, is not made of dimensionless Euclidean points nor of continuous mathematical lines but of distinct chunks of matter...) is then engaged as such, ideally, or in practice as close to its material structure as needed, with all of the apparent randomness and irregularity that will inevitably appear at each scale of resolution."[19] An example of this form of discreteness is found in the work 'Grotto' by Benjamin Dillenberger and Michael Hansmeyer, which uses the discrete manipulation of over 30 billion volumetric pixels, or voxels, to create extensive and immersive 3D printed environments.[20] Objects (including digital voxels and physical 3D prints) in this paradigm are allowed to affiliate, aggregate, and generate interstitial effects while maintaining varying degrees of individuality and autonomy.[21]

Through articulation, borders may be designed to relate outward yet into the surrounding environment as nested interiorities or surrounding objects may relate inward through borders of smaller objects. In the project "House on Ile Rene-Levasseur" by Mark Foster Gage Architects, the environment is designed and visualized as an object that the object of the house sits within. The work uses concepts of time as process to demonstrate the transgressive expansion of an objective, interiorized form of post-natural environment both onto and into the house-object . Through the object's own articulations, the living interiors of the environment interact locally, discretely, with the object. In the process, the border between object and environment is remade, and the object is almost, but not totally, subsumed into its environment, and the environment is literally informed through the object's articulations. The man-made and the natural are placed on the same footing in this operational model of nested interiority and articulated border. Therefore, the object maintains some autonomy and the overgrowth is also only partially 'natural'. The natural elements take on some of the aspects of the object conforming to its form while the object itself is partially

obscured in this direct interaction with its environment. This inherently follows the tenets of Object-Oriented Ontology while also developing discrete relations and notions of effects.

In another example from Professor Daniel Kohler's research at The Bartlett School of Architecture, discrete objects of everyday human habitation (bedrooms, living rooms, and kitchens, for example) proliferate extensively within objective urban environments. Kohler uses data to articulate and drive the local relations within this expanding set. He describes the process of moving from immaterial data to material objects as a form of urban transgression, stating that "today's abundant information inverses the foresight of an immaterialist city. The completed anthropomorphic scenography of our environments reverses as you look to its main driving ingredient. Data becomes the missing link between the human and inhuman parts of the city... ." [22]

In the B_Mu Tower proposed for Bangkok, Thailand by R&Sie(n), the architects propose another type of action, one that literally catalyzes microscopic polluting particles in the environment into larger forms as a phenomenotechnical experiment and a literal act of atmospheric scrubbing. [23] The work of materializing atmosphere at once creates form while also creating new types of action and interaction on the border between an object and the environment it is within.

The works outlined above are distinct visual and instrumental examples of object-based contextual actions which combine the spatial and ephemeral with the formal and particular to create articulate objects which generate new interiorized environments. However, "we are not accustomed to the idea that non-human,

inanimate objects possess agency and activity, just as we are not accustomed to the idea that they can carry information..."[24] These 'non-human' actors or objects (such as data, plants, or micro-pollutants) to which Easterling refers are, however, activated by the designer. Where B_Mu tower is acting on an interior urban atmosphere characterized by pollution, the existing contexts Kohler is acting within are defined not only by their relationship to forms of resistance in the codification of building, zoning, and land-use, but also through their relation to codes of capital flow as well as social and typological factors. Finally, Mark Gage's work invites an already interiorized form of designed nature, or post-nature, to interact with the object through the object's formal and material articulations. Transforming material and ephemeral information through design represents the greatest potential for developing new types of spatial ecologies within the varied scales of nested interiors that have been described.[25] Ultimately, in the process, objects (as interiorities, objects, and object-like environments nested within each other or within other systems) interact intensively without losing their autonomy.

Now that we are not only facing the reality of the Anthropocene but are also shifting to a post-human conceptual framework, we may be able to better understand the potential of nested discrete relations and forms of articulate interaction in new ways. This is certainly not idealized method and theory aimed toward the production of continuities or rigid resistance to existing forces. Instead, resistance is overturned by articulations of, variable relations between, and empathy for objects. In this way, design shifts to create effusive and proliferating identities which may allow all objects

RC8_WanderYards_Perspective_Landscape
(photo@ Daniel Koehler)

(including people) to exist and interact effectively with the constructions and contexts of the worlds that they either produce or are within.

Just as with codified hierarchies or Nolli's map, what we make also influences what we think. Emerging design processes, reinforced by conceptual and theoretical shifts, facilitate new actions and help develop new sensibilities, which are characterized by articulation, specificity, and connection. Ultimately, developing discrete forms and spatial articulations shows the potential to redistribute hierarchies and to supersede oppositional, resistance-based paradigms. Certainly, theoretical and instrumental modes of design are generating fresh models. These models focus on objects and interactions between object-based interiorities that have the capacity to aggregate at all scales, from particles to planets. Buckminster Fuller called it 'Spaceship Earth,' and we understand now that 'we are trapped, utterly reliant on our spaceship planet...' [26] Finally, these new ways of thinking and working may well generate even newer paradigms for action, productively synthesizing ecological thinking and empathetic imagining for a sustainable future inside.

ENDNOTES:

1 The notion of separation of mind and body, linked most explicitly to Descartes, may be at the core of this as a theoretical construct. Wikipedia, "Mind-body problem," Accessed Nov 14, 2017. https://en.wikipedia.org/wiki/Mind%E2%80%93body_problem

2 Philosopher and founder of the 'Sierra Club', John Muir is said to have said that "most people are on the world not in it."

3 Sean Lally, "When cold air sleeps," *Architectural Design* Issue 200, (07/2009): 56.

4 The Anthropocene is so named because of the effects individual, discrete human actions, in aggregate, are creating on a planetary scale.

5 Tom Roberts, "Thinking Technology for the Anthropocene: Encountering 3D Printing through the Philosophy of Gilbert Simondon," *Cultural Geographies* 24, no. 4 (2017): 540.

6 For a basic outline of Object Oriented Ontology see: Wikipedia, 'Object Oriented Ontology,' https://en.wikipedia.org/wiki/Object-oriented_ontology
For a basic outline of Post-Humanism see: WIkiPedia, 'Post-Humanism' https://en.wikipedia.org/wiki/Posthumanism .

7 The notion of the 'withdrawn' object is first posed by philosopher Graham Harman in his work, "Tool-Being: Elements in a Theory of Objects", and most often associated with his work and the general work of philosophy called Speculative Realism and Object Oriented Ontology. Graham Harman, *Tool-being: Heidegger and the Metaphysics of Objects* (Chicago: Open Court, 2002).

8 This builds on the notion of objects posed by philosopher Graham Harman, and associated with his work, and the associated philosophy called Object Oriented Ontology (OOO).

9 Timothy Morton, 'We have never been displaced," in *Olafur Eliasson: Reality Machines*, ed. Ólafur Elíasson and Matilda Olof-Ors (Stockholm: Modernamuseet, London; Koenig Books), 2015.

10 As a theoretical/philosophical position, we could say that what we typically understand as object's exterior may also be the inside the border of the interior we are already within.

11 The border as a uniform, hierarchical condition is being reconsidered today. For example, the type of border to which John Kerry is referring in his quote is often transcended by ephemeral actors from the destructive such as ideology-inspired terrorism to the more benign such as weather, flora and fauna. These transcendent actors, like ideas in the internet age, move freely between each country's interior.

12 David Ruy, "Returning to (Strange) Objects," *Tarp Architecture Manual*, (spring 2012):38-42.

13 Greg Lynn, "Intricacy," *Institute of Contemporary Art* (University of Pennsylvania: January 18-April 6, 2003).

14 Patrik Shumacher, "Parametricism," *Architectural Design 79*, no. 4 (2009): 14-23.

15 Mario Carpo, "Excessive Resolution," *Architectural Design* Issue 244, (06/2016): 81.

16 Timothy Morton, 'We have never been displaced," in *Olafur Eliasson: Reality Machines*, ed. Ólafur Elíasson and Matilda Olof-Ors (Stockholm: Modernamuseet, London; Koenig Books), 2015.

17 Tom Wiscombe, 'Discreteness, or Towards a Flat Ontology of Architecture," *Project*, Issue 3 (Spring 2014):35.

18 This builds on the notion of the 'withdrawn' object is posed by philosopher Graham Harman.
Graham Harman, *Tool-being: Heidegger and the Metaphysics of Objects* (Chicago: Open Court, 2002).

19 Mario Carpo, "Breaking the Curve" *Artforum International* Vol. 52, Iss. 6, (Feb 2014): 169-170,172-173.

20 "Digital Grotesque," Accessed Dec 1, 2017, https://digital-grotesque.com/architecture/

21 This notion of autonomy in relation to contingency (what is shared and what is 'withdrawn') is a tenet of OOO.

22 "Lab-Eds – RC8 2017 Wa(o)anderYards", Daniel Kohler, accessed Nov 20, 2017, http://www.lab-eds.org/Teaching-RC8-2017-Wa-o-anderYards.

23 'Phenomentechnique' is a reference to Gaston Bachelard's neo-logism regarding the need to conflate concept and object in science. "A natural science that suspects in can no longer get hold of the phenomena it is trying to track down by natural means has to produce in the first place those experiences it wants to investigate. Science thus become, first and foremost, a 'phenomena factory'." In Miriam Schaub, "The Logic of Light: Technology and the Humean Turn," in *Thyssen-Bornemisza Art Contemporary: The Collection Book,* ed by Eva Ebersberger and Daniela Zyman (Cologne: Walter KonigVerlag (2009), 139.
"B_Mu Tower," accessed Nov 10, 2017, http://www.new-territories.com/roche2002bis.htm

24 Keller Easterling, 'An Internet of Things,' *E-Flux Journal* #31 (Jan 2012). http://www.e-flux.com/journal/an-internet-of-things/14

25 I first made this analogy to media objects and interior urbanism in a paper presented at the Interiors Forum World Conference in Milan in May 2015.

26 David Bielo. *The Unnatural World* (New York: Scribner, 2016), 3.

KLAN KOSOVA

RESISTING NEW ORDER

by A S T R I T   N I X H A

The 'Klan KOSOVA' is one of the first examples of an industrial building transformation in Kosovo, converted from a 1980's shock absorber factory into a television studio. The transformation highlights a building's ability to give subliminal messages about the context of its materials, and generates an awareness about their reuse. Through the choice and narratives of the materials used, the building remembers, yells, screams, whispers, creates sanctuary, and absolves. It moralizes, redeems, and heals. In an act of defiance, it represents a resistance to the new social and political order of the place while looking to the future.

Once a typical industrial space defined by a sea of interior columns and continuous strip windows, the factory has been transformed to its new use primarily through an innovative reuse of abandoned materials – materials from the factory itself but also those abandoned due to political and social changes within the country. The architecture of the new television studio brings the old building and the recycled materials to new life, and also emphasizes and enhances the social pattern of its users. These characteristics bring a dynamic design that represents concepts of environmental, social and spiritual sustainability.

The 120-meter-long facade is clad in recycled railway sleepers

The reused materials imbue the shattered building structure with new meaning, as does the integration of recycled materials from various parts of Kosovo. The reuse of elements from the former factory, such as light fixtures, radiators, and pipes, not only retains the original manufacturing infrastructure, but also contributes accessory elements to the interior.

Reuse of solid waste from different parts of the country has a positive environmental impact, and serves as an example of how to create compelling architectonic expression. Most of the interior surfaces were built with recycled materials: bricks from the ruins of houses burned during the Kosovo War, wooden walls made out of refuse planks. The exterior was made with recycled railway sleepers' boards, composed in a natural parametric form in different sizes and dimensions.

It is a building that remembers. By using bricks from the ruins of houses burned during the Kosovo War to create an interior feature – a unique design that can be translated from the distress on the bricks themselves – the expression of Klan KOSOVA's building construction becomes something of an exclamation point. Through these visual traits we can understand its traumatic history: the shelling, the burning, and people's screams. Over 200,000 residential units were destroyed during the war. The need to rebuild the country as quickly as possible meant that there was not enough time to reconstruct from the existing ruins. Instead the country was built anew, leaving no reflective scar of its war throughout the countryside.

Muddied brick was extracted, cleaned and repositioned as the main interior walls, so that remembrance would become an aspect of everyday life without building a memorial. The bricks were laid with traditional

The original facade from the 1980s shock absorber factory before the transformation

Interior of the former shock absorber factory

mortar, 4 meters high and spanning 120 meters, on two floors. In specific cases, bricks were turned outside to represent the screams, the yelling, the gunfire and burning that they endured in their previous lives. The wall positively impacted the social economic context as well. The war rubble from the surrounding countryside was cleared to the extent that the project necessitated it, and poor families were given a modest amount of money as charity: about 10% of the bricks' market price. The largest impact that the construction of this wall enabled was the reevaluation, rebranding and reuse of local craftsmanship and design.

It is a building that screams its difference in presentation and style. Its façade is clad in recycled and cut railway sleepers. Every 20-25 years the railway changes the track sleepers, and despite the fact that the wood was treated with toxins for its original use, there was a time when the discarded material was burned and used for heating. When the European Union banned this process because of its toxic emissions, they legislated that the material be buried deep underground. The wood could therefore never find its reuse. This history gives the façade special meaning, as does the railway sleepers' role in expelling more than a million people during the war. Using safety provisions the façade incorporates the wood exactly as it came from the cut. The lifespan of the bolts and cuts is clearly rendered on the face of the building. 3-centimeter-thick planks of different sizes were fixed on the façade and made natural parametric designs on the site. The 120-meter-long façade proves that there is no such thing as waste, and that materials should be looked at anew in different contexts.

It is a building that whispers. Klan KOSOVA TV Station's slogan, "Klan Kosova - Jemi nje" (translated to "Klan KOSOVA – we're one"), is visible from the exterior through façade openings that graphically simulate sound waves. Windows are designed so that that the interior is flooded with an enormous amount of light.

It is a building that absolves through the reuse of the existing elements of the factory. Light fixtures, found hanging in the original building, were rehung. Transformers were cleaned, repainted, and electrically brought up to date by implementing a lighting scheme as a visible expression of the building's past use. This clean, retro application of the old elements is also visible in the reuse of the existing radiators and pipes from the original manufacturing infrastructure. Reused pipes were used in creating duct work for new electric infrastructure, radiators, and also, as desk legs.

It is a building that moralizes with respect to architecture. It presents a different approach to globalization. Its use of local, natural materials prompts discussions on environmentalism and wellbeing. Elements reflect wellbeing through local craftsmanship, the arts, and its materialization. It adds important questions about technological achievement in our time.

The interior use of bricks from the ruins of houses burned during the
Kosovo War

It is a building that redeems one way of living and questions another: Have we become artists who make design decisions that are only driven by time, and the requirements of the global building industry? Have we lost our sense of enjoyment during the work? Have we lost touch with time, and are our days becoming shorter and shorter? Are we losing the power to create by finding the easy way out? Have we become a society of homogenous personalities, reflected in global architecture, or is there a unique DNA to each of us? Klan KOSOVA redeems individuality, presented through recycled materials and design, and the scars embedded therein.

It is a building that heals wounds of ordinary, everyday life. It acknowledges that everything has a potential for recycle and reuse. It represents hope that life can be seen in different ways, and that these multifaceted perspectives should drive societies.

It is an act of defiance to globalization, in an effort to reclaim personality. It represents a resistance to the new order, while looking to the future. With architecture, we can make a stand and architecture can represent resistance to political and social order. Architecture can and will eventually drive social requirements to political approvals to a more humanly and environmentally friendly approach.

I believe that life is perfect because of its imperfection. That is why perfect architecture is expressed in buildings that reflect life's imperfections.

ENDNOTES:
1 200.000 represent destroyed apartments and houses. The number represents the figure of families not being able to shelter themselves after the war being one apartment or one house.

Reuse of existing elements from the factory, such as these light fixtures, heating radiators and pipes

THE PAST EMBODIED IN ACTION

by LAURA GIOENI

Space is not merely a geometrical issue and a pure dimensional entity given before the body and its movement. This important lesson came not from my architectural studies, but from the theatrical school, based in the methods of Jacques Lecoq, where I trained as actor and mime. That idea remained long submerged in my unconscious until it soared free, clear and distinct, during my philosophical studies. It is summarized by Ludwig Wittgenstein's observation that "architecture is a gesture" and that "not every purposive movement of the human body is a gesture. Just as little as every functional building is architecture." [1]

Unlike other arts, architecture addresses itself not only to our sight but to our whole body, configuring itself, so to speak, as the double rebound of our gestures. As almost an extension of our body, architecture becomes its further limit, the reflecting surface where body and the world simultaneously mirror themselves; in pragmatic terms we can say that the authentic meaning of architecture resides exactly in our practical replay, in what architecture invites us to do. In this way, architecture reveals its deeper sense and makes us connect to a building's past. The architectural environment activates our physical response, linking us to the chain of gestures of its designers, builders and tenants through material

The remains of the first two lateral chapels of the XVII century and the angular columns of the pronaos of the temple, embedded in the new glass facade, delimit a kind of open vestibule to the cathedral

traces left behind. Every modification provides the existing building with new interpretations that constitute its evolving authenticity, historical value and meaning.

Referring to architecture as "mimesis of the body" in his seminal book, *The Eyes of the Skin*, Juhani Pallasmaa argues that "architecture is communication from the body of the architect directly to the body of the person who encounters the work, perhaps centuries later."[2] Referencing Henri Bergson's research, Pallasmaa reminds us that "there is an inherent suggestion of action in images of architecture, the moment of active encounter, or a «promise of function» and purpose," a possibility of action which implies a "bodily reaction as inseparable aspect." As designers and users, this bodily experience of architecture is linked to our memory. In the "Lamp of Memory," John Ruskin remarked that our faculty of remembering relies on architecture. In a similar way, Pallasmaa observes that "the body knows and remembers. Architectural meaning derives from archaic responses and reactions remembered by the body and the senses."[3] Thus, "a meaningful architectural experience is not simply a series of retinal images" and architectural elements are not only visual components, but "confrontation that interacts with memory."[4]

Reflecting on the interplay between memory, body and act, Edward Casey underlines the role of "body memory" as the "natural center of any sensitive account of remembering,"[5] as privileged point of view able to illuminate the nature of our relationship with the past. He defines "habitual body memory," as a pre-reflective, tacit and pre-articulate dimension of human experience, where the remembering resides just in the performance of actions. Casey reflects that "in such memory the past is embodied in action. Rather than being contained separately somewhere in the mind or brain, it is actively an ingredient in the very bodily movements that accomplish

View from the naos of the Temple of Augustus towards the remains of the choir and apse of the Baroque church of Saint Proculus

The new marble altar and ambo dialogue with the remains of the
classical monument

a particular action." [6]   Likewise, architectural design, far before its drawn expression, arises from this interplay of body and memory. Speaking from experience, this is one of the most interesting offspring of Lecoq's theatrical pedagogy when applied to architectural teaching.

Jacques Lecoq is one of the most influential pedagogues of modern theatre. Nevertheless, his contribution to architectural education is little known and quite underestimated. Lecoq began to apply his research on mime, gesture and movement to architectural pedagogy in 1968, when he was invited to teach at the École Nationale Supérieure des Beaux-Arts in Paris: since then and for over 20 years, he developed a mimodynamic approach to the training of architects. Lecoq's pedagogy focused on the fundamental relationship between architectural space and body movement and gestures, investigated through the miming practice. His method is based on the study of movement, embodiment and improvisation. Lecoq conceived of miming as a universal background for our relationship with the world, as knowledge process that leads to the rediscovery of the dynamic meaning of life. Mimodynamic method represents a universal pedagogical tool, useful not only for actor training but, in general, in every field of knowledge, including architecture: "every true artist is a mime." - Lecoq writes - "Picasso's ability to draw a bull depended on his having found the *essential* Bull in himself, which released the shaping gesture of his hand. He was miming. Painters and sculptors are outstanding mime artists because they share in the same act of embodiment (...). This is why I could move from teaching theatre to teaching architecture, and how I invented «architect-mimes»." [7]

In the architectural field, Lecoq aimed to improve the design skills of architects: to build in a better way means to consider the dynamics of the body and its movements. According to Lecoq, architectural education, like every other form of artistic training, should always be founded on bodily awareness. Only through the involvement of the point of view of the body in the observation of reality and by means of the embodiment of creative process, can one reach what he called "the universal poetic sense." [8] The moving body is intended by Lecoq as the center of a space-time interrelation projecting a field of forces and creating the space. Every gesture played by human beings happens in a relationship with the space around them. The external space is reflected in the inner space, provoking an emotional feeling and a motor response. The natural and the built environment mime themselves in us and make us move. Lecoq's pedagogy shows in practice the body as the mirroring margin of the world and architecture as the living threshold between our gestures and the environment.

The creative process springs from a narrative bodily action, starting from the interplay of the present of the situation and the past of the memory, so that "the

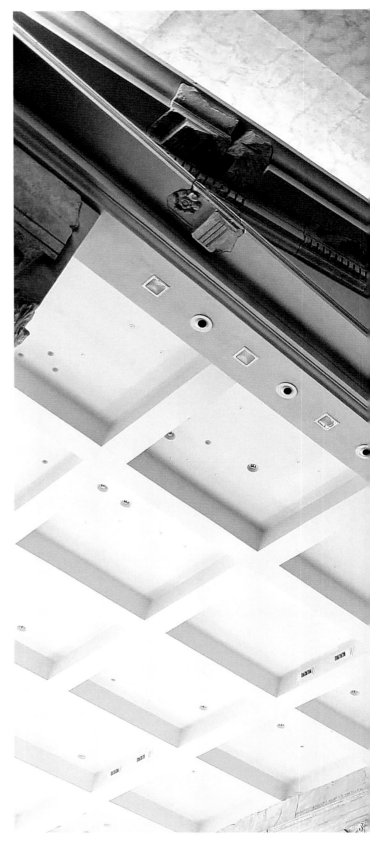

The gap between the reconstructed rear pediment of the temple and the
lunette vault of the baroque chancel

dynamics of the memory are more important than the memory itself." Lecoq writes that when one is confronted with a new place for the first time, "suddenly memory is triggered (...); you are in an image of the present and suddenly an image of the past appears. Out of the interplay between these two images comes the improvisation." [9]

These bodily roots of memory as action emerge in our natural mimodynamic embodiment of the world and constitute the fundamentals of the architectural design process and the architects' drawing gesture. In consonance with Lecoq's teaching, Pallasmaa underlines that "the making of architecture (...) is a specific embodied mode of thought that takes place through the sense and the body" and configures architecture as "projection of the human body and its movement through space." [10] According to Pallasmaa, we need to understand the space in terms of dynamic interactions: "basic architectural experiences have a verb form rather than being nouns." [11]

The mimodynamic origin of architecture, involving body and memory in action, shows its haptic dimension in opposition to its characterization as immaterial and "retinal." Likewise, bodily and gestural dimension plays the main role in the architectural design process, when the drawing action of the "thinking hand" designs, cuts, incises, decides, and starts to trace limits between the domain of possible and the kingdom of necessity.

Corinthian capitals emerged from the walls of the Baroque church after the fire which ravaged the building in 1964

Focusing on this gesture, Pallasma explains how the natural hand-eye-mind connection works in drawing, when the tip of the pencil becomes almost an extension of fingerprints and a bridge between mental and physical space.

This phenomenological approach to the architecture and design process, which accords the greatest importance to the dynamics of the body, gestures and actions, shares with pragmatism the same concept of meaning as "purpose of action." This leads to a reconsideration, together with the traditional idea of meaning and space, of the classical concept of time, in a renewed attitude towards history and historical heritage, taking into account the dynamic nature of our relationship with the past. Following Friedrich Nietzsche and Michel Foucault, this new perspective can be called Genealogy. Genealogy embraces a hermeneutical view towards the issue of temporality: past, present and future do not constitute a simple succession of atomic unrelated instants, rather they are in a circle where the past, according to Heidegger, is waiting at the gateway of the future. So, a genealogical approach recognizes the hermeneutical and projecting character of the memory, which, in architecture, as memory in act, is activated through a chain of bodily actions and reactions between designer and user.

The authentic and living meaning of history resides in how we respond and correspond to the past in a practical act, a behavior, a habit. In this way, even historical monuments lose the eternal present of their origin, acquiring a new sense as a (re)collection of the chain of their interpretations. Certainly, intervention on existing architecture must grow from respect for authentic material components, from which the architecture also takes, in a broad sense, its historic value, and its identity; but, at the same time, we have to acknowledge that usefulness is part of architectural meaning and identity. Use forms part of the identity of architecture: an identity which is not invariable and changes according to the transformations of its past by a memory which, as interpretation and project, looks and aims to the future.

The case of the conservation and reuse of the temple-cathedral in Pozzuoli, Naples is an expression of the ideas above: one of many acts over time, mediating identity through continuous use over millennia.

When, in 2004, the professional team led by Marco Dezzi Bardeschi won the international contest for the restoration of the ruined temple cathedral, the palimpsest communicated, in the polyphonic and fragmented state of anatomic dissection, an incomparable documental and emotional richness. I was a member of the team entrusted with the ruin. The building told us of its three main archaeological layers: the first composed of relics of the Republican Roman Capitolium and Temple of Augustus; the second, the ruin of the Christian cathedral with the Baroque Holy Sacrament Chapel and Chapter Hall; finally, the third layer exhibited the scars from a destructive and unfinished intervention undertaken in 1968, aimed at reconstructing the Roman temple after a devastating fire in 1964. Further, the site and surrounding urban context were emptied of inhabitants after an earthquake and continued seismic activity during the 1980s.

The project team faced two main tasks. On one hand, we rejected any aspiration to re-establish the lost formal unity of the original building, and instead focused on guaranteeing the legibility of the historical document in its complex material stratification; on the other hand, we aimed at bringing life to the site through two seemingly opposite goals, cultic and cultural: providing

Corinthian half column of the pseudo-peristyle emerges in the gap between
the wall of the temple and the Holy Sacrament Chapel

the monument with reuse as a place of religious worship aimed at a social and urban level, and creating a living cultural center as museum and archaeological site.

In places the conservation project leaves fragments and discontinuities, which, as stones on a path, make the memory stumble, while elsewhere contemporary elements complete broken forms, which, as polished terrazzo, make the memory slide into the now.

Thus, structural glass walls, with the silhouettes of the destroyed columns of the pronaos, the new bell tower, which hosts three historic bronze bells, the new inclined floor of the cella, almost a theater parterre with site-specific wooden furniture, interact with the ancient remains and act as invitation to use, as suggestion of action, as gesture, pushing to enter, sit down, walk around, look at the sky, and discover, in these bodily attitudes, the past embodied in action.

ENDNOTES:

1 Ludwig Wittgenstein, *Culture and Value: A Selection from the Posthumous Remains*, 2nd Ed. (Oxford & Malden: Blackwell Publishers,1998), 149.

2 Juhani Pallasmaa, *The Eyes of the Skin: Architecture and the Senses*. (Hoboken: Wiley, 2005), 67.

3 Pallasmaa, 60.

4 Pallasmaa, 63.

5 E.S. Casey, *Remembering: A phenomenological Study*. (Bloomington: Indiana University press, 2000), 148.

6 Casey, 149.

7 J.G. Carasso, J. Lecoq, and J.C. Lallias J, *The Moving Body: Teaching Creative Theatre* 2nd Ed. (London & New York: Bloomsbury, 2002), 23.

8 Carasso, Lecoq and Lallias, 5.

9 Carasso, Lecoq and Lallias, 31.

10 Pallasmaa, 44-45.

11 Pallasmaa, 63.

A floor raised to its original height connects the lower level of the chancel which hosts the seats for the faithful

FREE SPEECH COMES HOME

LA CASA DEL HIJO DEL AHUIZOTE

by ENRIQUE SILVA

Freedom of speech, freedom of conscience, freedom of assembly; abolition of slavery and of the death penalty; freedom of the press: these and other fundamental individual rights were granted to citizens by the liberal Federal Constitution of the United Mexican States of 1857. [1] Sadly, the promises of the document would never fully come to fruition. By the 46th anniversary of this same Constitution, leftist intellectuals and political activists united against the totalitarian government established by General Porfirio Díaz. Among these protestors were Ricardo, Enrique and Jesús Flores Magón, who would rise to prominence as voices of change for Mexico. The General ruled as dictator of Mexico for 31 years, enforced strict censorship of all political opposition, and was ousted only by the Mexican Revolution of 1910.

The brief period during which the Flores Magón brothers ran the satirical newspaper *El Hijo del Ahuizote* proved meteoric for the rhetoric of the Revolution to come, giving words to the fight for democracy. Originally founded 1895, *El Hijo del Ahuizote* used the political cartoon as a vehicle to spread "fierce and independent political opposition against everything that is wrong," [2] taking aim at all levels of government, from the General to state governors, congressmen and the church. It was both a source of news and direct critique that could be understood by all levels of Mexican society, even those who were illiterate. The newspaper's printing headquarters became the stage for one of the most important moments for the history of freedom of the press and democracy in Mexico on February 5th, 1902.

The Centro Documental Flores Magón, A.C. consists of more than 15,000 documents and 35,000 images, stored in moveable furniture designed by Giacomo Castagnola

© Roberto Arellano

TOP

THE CONSTITUTION HAS DIED draped across the façade of the El Hijo del
Ahuizote printing house on February 5th, 1902

BOTTOM

The same view today: commercial use by local vendors keeps the
streetscape alive, with archive above

THE CONSTITUTION HAS DIED was draped across the façade in bold letters. The banner was accompanied by an incendiary essay and subsequent critical publications against the censorship of the regime, prompting the forced dissolution of *El Hijo del Ahuizote* and the exile that pushed the Flores Magón brothers across the border to the United States. The brothers remained politically active remotely; from Laredo, Texas and Los Angeles, California among other border-state cities, the binational narrative became an important aspect of both the political resistance and the private life of the Flores Magón family. This involvement continued through successive generations.

The 19th-century building that housed *El Hijo del Ahuizote* sits within the Santo Domingo neighborhood of downtown Mexico City, an area deeply affected by decentralization policies and urban development strategies that led to sprawl during the 1940s and 50s. The construction of the National University Campus on the southern outskirts of the capital pulled academics away from downtown, and the transfer of Federal Agencies to less congested parts of the city caused the gradual decline of the neighborhood. La Casa del Hijo del Ahuizote, alongside other historic buildings without explicit touristic appeal, was abandoned. Expropriated by the federal government after the earthquake that struck Mexico City in 1985 and disused for decades, the historic structure was completely dilapidated: the interiors destroyed, the facade stripped of ornamentation, the windows filled with brick.

Change came at the turn of the 21st century, when Mexico City's historic downtown underwent multimillion dollar public-private urban renewal efforts. A side effect of this work was the widespread relocation of street vendors into publicly owned buildings like the *El Hijo del Ahuizote* printing house, in order to improve urban mobility.

When the grandson of Enrique Flores Magón, Diego Flores Magón, presented an adaptive reuse project to the Historic Center Authority in 2007, it was clear the architectural and cultural aspects of the design had to incorporate the interests of all stakeholders, from the residents of Santo Domingo to street vendors to the Flores Magón Archive. The building that had housed one of the most liberal voices of resistance against authoritarianism a hundred years ago had to democratically engage with its community in order to be rescued. An act of intervention through negotiation was required: the Casa del Hijo del Ahuizote was born.

The cultural center envisioned by Diego Flores Magón was developed with three directives:

First, an archive for the Centro Documental Flores Magón, A.C. (The Flores Magón Documentary Center) with facilities for exhibition. Consisting of more than 15,000 documents and 35,000 images, the archive preserves the Flores Magón ideals and presents them to the general public. Thanks to a grant from Harvard University, the archive has been digitized, allowing access without the need of appointment or academic credentials to explore and learn about the Flores Magóns' role in Mexico's political history.

Second, to provide a place for the binational artistic community of Mexicans, Americans and Mexican-Americans to meet on a regular basis and maintain dialogue on issues relevant to both sides of the border, particularly relating to Magonismo, the arnarcho-communist school of thought that led to the Mexican revolution of 1910. It is in this context that the Casa del Hijo del Ahuizote relation to the Chicano-Pocho / Mexican-American duality becomes essential to the success of the cultural project. In addition, an annual residency for an artist or academic allows use of gallery space on the second floor to curate border related exhibitions.

Third, to establish the Casa del Hijo del Ahuizote as a live laboratory of critical journalism, offering spaces for seminars, workshops and research related to both the history of Mexican press and to contemporary independent publication efforts. In the words of collaborator María del Mar Gámiz Vidiella," in each of these activities the juxtaposition between archive, history and everyday life becomes apparent, allowing for a democratic critique of official narratives to be explored in the flexible rooms and high ceilings of the Casa del Hijo del Ahuizote." [3]

If the Casa del Hijo del Ahuizote was to succeed, the compromise between local authorities and street vendors must also support community engagement in order to become an integral part of Santo Domingo. From the very beginning these goals influenced the intervention strategy. The first floor of the three story building and open ground space were left for commercial use by local vendors, while the archive and gallery spaces were placed on the second and third floors. A single entrance allows access for all and leads to a lobby hung with a photo of the historic 1902 protest, creating collective space between the cultural center, the vendors and the visitors.

A new wood and steel self-bearing staircase and moveable furniture designed by industrial designer Giacomo Castagnola mark the intervention, as well as the restoration of the street facade and incorporation of a public rooftop terrace. The furniture that was designed for the third floor includes continuous archival storage around the perimeter of the building and a folding, moveable workspace. A digital printing machine recalls the printing tradition, both in intellectual production and in the physical layout of the space, while a piece for the storage of paper completes the design. According to Castagnola, the furniture for la Casa del Hijo del Ahuizote mixes historic principles of anarchism such as mutual help and spontaneous creativity. Flexibility in arrangement and the ability to fold much of the furniture

away relates the intervention to the street furniture utilized for informal commerce by the street vendors below.[4]

Restoration efforts undertaken by local authorities in Mexico City's historic downtown are viewed by locals as potential threats because of the complex relationship between public-private investment, gentrification and tourism. In addition to negotiation efforts between the archive, local authorities and the street vendors, it was imperative to the success of the project to engage residents of Santo Domingo; underprivileged and ignored by authorities for generations, the neighborhood developed strong social and identity ties. Casa del Hijo del Ahuizote needed not only to serve as an archive, but to bring access to educational resources and a sense of pride to Santo Domingo. Navigating the mistrust of residents wary of gentrification, the project was positioned as a cultural resource, not a destination meant for tourists but a place for local engagement and education.

In order to encourage participation from residents, the Casa del Hijo del Ahuizote partnered with Génesis Flores Rojas to spearhead an engagement program. Génesis, daughter of merchants herself, had frequented the area for years and was familiar both with the site and surrounding community. Anthropologist by training, she served as the interpreter between the Flores Magón

Versatile in arrangement and storage options, the furniture relates to carts utilized for informal commerce by street vendors, like this elote seller seen from above

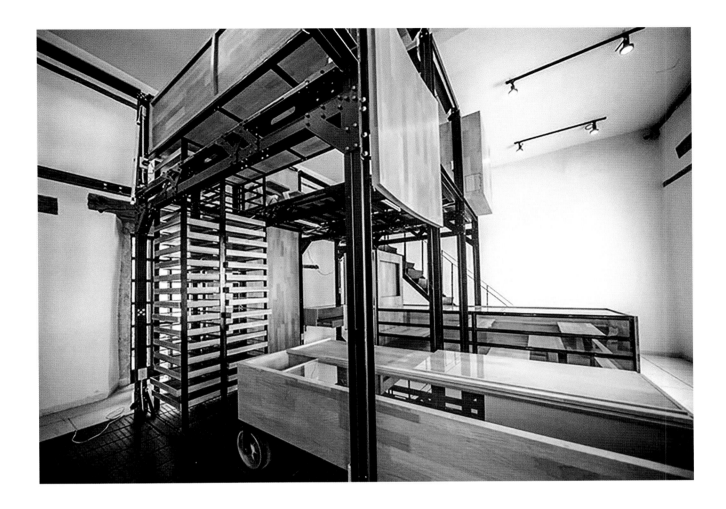

project and neighbors in Santo Domingo.[5] With the implementation of several educational workshops for children and families around traditional arts and crafts practices, locals were tempted to interact with the cultural center, with its "foreign" visitors, with the local merchants and with other families of the neighborhood. The act of rebuilding the urban ruin and of preserving the archival materials was complemented with the inclusion of the neighborhood families as participants.

This social coexistence is central to the ideology and built environment of the Casa del Hijo del Ahuizote, living up to the mission statement to "stand with the purpose of building mutual beneficial relations between the Flores Magón Archive and the Santo Domingo neighborhood....by means of a cultural center that explores freedom and the rethinking of borders, located in the antique house of *El Hijo del Ahuizote*."[6]

A present-day beacon of political critique, social engagement, cultural conscience and democratic inclusion, la Casa del Hijo del Ahuizote continues to open its doors for the academic researcher, the motivated artist, the neighborhood child and the casual passerby alike.

Standing as a promoter for freedom of the press within the third deadliest country to be a journalist in the world, the work of Diego and the memory of the Flores Magon's struggle is as relevant today as 116 years ago.

ENDNOTES:

1 H. N. Rowe Branch. "L. S. The Mexican Constitution of 1917 Compared with The Constitution of 1857, "*The Annals of the American Academy of Political and Social Science*, Vol. 71, Supplement (May, 1917), pp. i-v+1-116

2 F. Belmont. "El hijo del Ahuizote" en *la Revolución Mexicana. Cultura Colectiva – Historia*. 14/11/2013

3 M. Gámiz. "Arquitectura de la memoria, La Casa del Hijo del Ahuizote. " *Limulus*. Online Journal.

4 G. Castagnola. "La Casa del Hijo del Ahuizote. Arquitectura de exposición." giacomocastagnola.com

5 M. Gámiz. "Arquitectura de la memoria, La Casa del Hijo del Ahuizote." *Limulus*. Online Journal.

6 https://issuu.com/casadelahuizote

Movement and action characterize the Archive's Storage, with the intent to recall historic principles of anarchism such as mutual help and spontaneous creativity

EMPOWERING ACTIONS

THE PARTICIPATORY RENOVATION OF A SHELTER

by CRISTIAN CAMPAGNARO AND NICOLÒ DI PRIMA

Action and spatiality

What does it mean to act within a space? And acting on a space with the clear intent of transforming it? We should firstly consider that not only subjects act on spaces but, in turn, spaces act on those subjects that traverse and inhabit them. "The meaning of a space lies in its effect on any objects that come into contact with it and which, while trying to alter the space, end up being transformed themselves." [1] As semiologist Gianfranco Marrone states, spaces and subjects share an indissolubly reciprocal relationship: space-object connection is always characterized by a need for narrative, meaning that – on the connotation level – both the space and the object may function alternatively as subject and object. [2] Thus, a space, far from being static and unchangeable, must in fact be considered an actor, able to control the behaviour of any objects that interact with it. When considering a space, we must think of it not merely as a physical entity, but also – and above all – as a conveyor of meaning. Understanding a space means "rediscovering the human intervention behind the objects of the world that has in fact given them sense." [3] In other words, the sense of a place is not given unequivocally (though it may be foreseen and planned) but rather it is continually ascribed by the very subject or subjects inhabiting it; furthermore, it can also change over time. We can therefore affirm that not only does a subject produce (both physically and semantically) the space – and the physical objects that constitute it – but also that spaces produce subjects.

In our everyday lives, this process occurs silently and imperceptibly. Referring to Goffman's frames theory, [4] anthropologist Daniel Miller states that "material objects are a setting. They make us aware of what

The 1st floor hall after the collaborative renovation process

is appropriate and inappropriate [...] They work most effectively when we don't actually look at them." [5] He defines this property as the humility of things: their silent presence produces a normalising (and normative) effect on the context. In this consists the very subjectivising power of the space. Simply by staying in place, its constituting objects produce in individuals a sense of familiarity with their surroundings, a sense of habitual normality which helps the living being to define, decipher and recognise the environment around them.

This mechanism is generally reassuring and reduces cognitive overload; it produces that feeling of "home" which allows individuals to inhabit a space "naturally," somewhere they can carry out their activities without feeling continuously out of place. Since the physical stability of a space is directly linked to the stability of its connotation, the "humility of things" also suggests that places function the more static and unchangeable they are.

But when the connotation ascribed to a space by an individual is unclear or not shared, he feels out of his element, uncomfortable in his surroundings. He feels excluded from the context, immobilised or perhaps he even has a desire to escape. In these cases, the "humble" immobility of spaces partly inhibit the idea of acting on a space, in order to transform and align it more with the connotation desired by the individual or the community inhabiting it. This means that the individual ends up suffering in the space around him.

The humility of objects (and, we could add, of places) is therefore concurrently reassuring – in regard to our more habitual daily activities – and inhibiting, compared to more transformative actions.

The shelter: a space with no action
This theoretical introduction will help us interpret the case study we present herein, referring to a particular type of space in which the freedom of its inhabitants' actions (daily and transformative) is particularly inhibited.

Since 2009 our interdisciplinary research-group, composed of designers from Polytechnic of Turin and anthropologists from University of Turin, works in the field of homelessness in several Italian cities. [6] The research reflects on the power of places to define the wellness of people that inhabit them and looks at the way in which spaces and objects interact with the stories of users and with the educational actions of social workers. [7]

From the very beginning, the research aimed at interlinking analysis with concrete actions that could have tangible effects on the spaces for the guests and those working therein as social workers, therefore establishing itself as an action research.

Concrete actions are, in fact, a useful analytical tool in reaching more in-depth understanding of the institutional policies and mechanisms that regulate housing systems as well as stimulating immediate improvement within the contexts of study. They are also a way of understanding if and how such contexts and their inhabitants are able to take on board, or even sustain, the transformations generated by the interventions.

On the conceptual level shelters seem to correspond with those that Michel Foucault defines heterotopias. [8] The shelter is a heterotopic space as, though in appearance it resolves the issue of someone who has lost home (due to economic, health and/or migratory issues), at the same time it contributes to labelling him as deviant. The function of the shelter in our society is strongly influenced by the fact that the housing crisis is interpreted as deviant but also as an emergency, leading welfare institutions to think (and hope) that the situation may be as temporary as possible.

Access to these structures is not based on the desire of individuals but is regulated by our welfare system, through strict institutional procedures. Those inhabiting these places are, in a certain sense, banned. [9] The shelter is, therefore, an "other space," one that enjoys a marginal (and often marginalising) relationship with the "normality" into which it is inserted, thus generating extreme physical and psychological suffering among inhabitants. They are places which, despite having a specific raison d'être (to accommodate those in difficulty), produce an inflexion that may prove destabilising for inhabitants: "I'm here (because I have no other choice), but I wish not to be here." Inhabited only by 'guests,' these are places that generate a sense of perennial exclusion and permanent temporariness. [10] These factors greatly inhibit the individuals' freedom of action within the space, not only how they use it but – even more so – in that they cannot make even the slightest alteration to their environment.

The space of the shelter, furthermore, produces exclusion, marginality and a sense of temporariness not only due to its functional systems (rules, curfews, and rights of access) but also through its physical characteristics. Buildings that host shelters are rarely designed for that function. Generally speaking, they are buildings constructed for specific purposes (schools, offices, factories) which, once their original function ceases, are temporarily transformed into housing. In other cases, due to the presumed temporariness and state of emergency of the service, basic prefabs are used. Furthermore, on the topographic level, buildings that are identified for this use tend to be found in the suburbs of cities and/or in so-called "social" districts which often are already populated by low-income or poor inhabitants and by a high percentage of immigrant residents. Finally, these buildings are often in a state of almost-complete abandonment and manifest rather serious structural problems and yet, despite this, they are used for housing purposes.

In these cases, reuse would appear to be counter-productive as renovations can prove extremely costly (due to the evident structural incompatibility between the old and new functions) but also because, given the urgency, rarely are the renovations completed before the inhabitants move in. Often, in fact, renovations are carried out when the service has already started and further complications inevitably arise.

Finally, there is also the risk that effective renovation works cannot be fully completed either because the (council or state-owned) building is protected by architectural regulations aimed at preserving the historical authenticity thereof, or because they are not considered to be a sufficiently profitable investment for the (non-state) organisation granted the contract for the short-term housing service and commissioned to manage the premises. Additionally, we cannot ignore the effect that this option has on public expenditure in terms of added costs. Management of a service supplied in places that are inefficient, from the perspective of the provision of welfare services, implies an extraordinary consumption of personal and material resources that could otherwise be avoided.

All these aspects basically allude to the fact that any chance of modifying and renovating these spaces is, though vital, in no way aided.

Action as a relationship

Based on the theoretical scenario briefly introduced in the first part of the article (which looks in-depth at the functioning of reciprocity in the space-subject connection) and the empirical observation of housing carried out by the Turin research group (of which we have highlighted some elements of analysis emerging from both on the semantic and physical-spatial level) we can understand how the transformative processes may appear simultaneously delicate and complicated.

In order to better understand these processes, we hereby present the case study of a collaborative project to renovate a Milanese shelter in which our research group has been involved for over two years now. In

The making of one of the benches that will be installed in via Mambretti 33, during the workshop "goBENCHING", attended also by a group of design students from the Polytechnic of Turin

December 2013, the Council of Milan granted Fondazione Progetto ARCA Onlus a twenty-year lease without charge of the former school building in Via Mambretti 33. Immediately, the building housed more than 250 people, including homeless adults and asylum seekers. The lease included all systems to be updated, and the structure to be renovated and furnished for housing purposes. Located in the Quarto Oggiaro district the building was constructed in the early 1900s and stands out for its neo-Classical style typical of early-20th century public buildings in Italy. The structure extends over three floors, each of around 1,200 m2 and its unusual "C" shape gives it a courtyard of around 760 m2. Its façades have, by now, completely eroded. The marble entrance hall contains a majestic central double stairway. Each floor contains a number of spacious, well-illuminated rooms opening onto straight, naturally-lit corridors which have since been set up as bedrooms for its current function. It is an enormous and imposing building whose initial magnificence only emphasizes

Some of the corridors at the end of the collaborative renovation process, with a co-constructed bench in foreground

renovation work was to be undertaken in close collaboration with and including the building's inhabitants (both beneficiaries and providers of the service) in all procedures, from selection and planning all the way through to execution.

We used the need to transform the spaces as a chance to activate the occupants. The collaborative approach emerged from the idea that, in order to be effective and recognised by the inhabitants themselves, the planning or re-planning of housing should involve them directly. The interventions undertaken, therefore, do not merely aim towards the realisation of the same but rather to encourage the users to act, taking on board the aspirations, needs and abilities of each individual. From consultation to co-planning to the co-production of the service, the project has involved the expertise of current and future inhabitants – guests, social operators, Foundation managers and, in future, the inhabitants of the district – in designing suitable forms of housing and the effective processes and tools for putting them into practice.

Preparations were characterised by the use of some qualitative research tools, such as ethnography, in-depth interviews, semi-structured interviews, focus groups, "guided" tours of some of the Foundation's housing and a comparative analysis thereof. During this phase, we surveyed the living and working needs of the various people affected by the project and also their knowledge and skills, so that the final project may utilise the practical and theoretical contribution of all and be subscribed to and recognised by as many of the group as possible. This analysis brought us to the strategies for renovating the spaces, mitigating as many living and working difficulties as possible which increasingly distinguish the very intent of the project.

The objectives of the collaborative activities are:

- To re-interpret: re-read and re-configure the spaces of the structure, best utilising the building's most characteristic structural features, while in line with whatever constraints have been placed on its transformation. Experimentations consisted in reinforcing the communal areas aimed at socialising and daily activities.

- To equip: furnish the spaces with equipment that is (both in quality and quantity) suitable for the functions assigned to them. Flexible seating systems, multiple mobile phone recharging points, way-finding systems and waste disposal systems of suitable capacity.

- To involve: experiment in cooperation with the operators and guests, utilising people's skills and aspirations, in order to promote care and attention to the spaces and equipment.

- To bring together: involve citizens in activities, promoting a non-stigmatised approach to and knowledge of the residents.

today's decline, partly the natural effect of the decades that have passed since it was built, but also due to a more gradual decay.

In order to transform the former school into housing, in 2015 the foundation commissioned our research group to scientifically supervise the overall development of the renovations project. The project was called "Cantiere Mambretti." [11]

As with the other experiments carried out by our group in other Italian cities, the idea was that any

The workshop as a tool of collective action

Collaborative planning as a process includes moments of analysis and research and is characterised by scrupulous moments of observation and inspection. These are alternated with other briefer and more intense moments in which reflection and planning pave the way for onsite experimentation, inspection and collective action.

One of the most effective devices that action-research has used is the temporary workshop, an experience of union and reciprocity. As we have verified in this and previous case studies, the idea of transforming space struggles to be consistent with the ordinary time of daily life. Yet the context of workshop, thanks to its extraordinary nature, can enable this idea. According to this, workshops become extraordinary events in which the entire group of inhabitants is ideally and practically invited to participate in the transformation. They are events that create "spaces" of participation and collaborative reflection between all interested parties, generating a dimension of enthusiasm, curiosity and creativity.

The workshop itself is preceded by tangible planning proposals which are, in fact, elaborated by the research group interlinking the data acquired from the qualitative research (bottom-up) with the needs of the managing organisation (top-down). The technical designs and study models are discussed with the service operators and with the building's most permanent inhabitants,

aimed at gradually refining the proposals. Once the project has been negotiated and defined, we pass on to the experimental dimension of the workshop, aimed at collectively and collaboratively undertaking the enterprise together with the beneficiaries of the service. In this context, we focus on the execution and preparatory techniques: quick, simple activities to involve all those who wish to participate, whether or not they have any experience of the theme in question; however, it should be clarified that this does not mean that the final result is of poor quality. Indeed, all the co-design and co-construction processes are strongly managed by designer and researcher from the point of view of outputs and outcomes.

The images of the workshop give the idea of how the execution of every project - from wall painting to production of benches - is the result of this rich and dynamic cooperation between designers and guests. It is a process of mutual learning in which sometimes guests learn from designers and conversely guests teach designers and other participants.

Action and housing

The collaborative experience is still ongoing and has not been without risks. Firstly, we have witnessed how the occupants have to be continually stimulated to participate in discussing the themes in question. The very complexity of the place and the social relationships that

A moment from the "ColorFULL Workshop": a series of workshops aimed to repaint common spaces of the building

are generated therein slow the transformative process. One serious problem consists in the (real and perceived) temporariness that reverberates not only in the management and transformation of the spaces, but which also characterises the perspective of the individual in regard to the (again, real or perceived) permanence of stay in the shelter. The workshop is able to arouse curiosity and cooperation, but this tends to remain circumscribed within the workshop as a singular event.

With respect to the social workers, on the other hand, our challenge is keeping them focussed on the management and transformation of the spaces. Burdened as they are by the arduous educational work that they are required to provide, they demonstrate a propensity to delegate to the research group for anything non-educational.

If it is so that this situation determines a modest decline in transformative effectiveness (in terms of time rather than quality), it must however be noted to what extent the collaborative transformation process increases its effectiveness: by understanding that concrete action immediately and perceptively influences the place in which they live, an individual's focus on elements that are of direct interest to him is catalysed and renewed regularly. And it is precisely this matter that we should use as a launch-pad to create moments of inclusion characterised by debate, discussion and a sharing of knowledge and to some way encourage direct action by the occupants themselves.

We have observed that reusing spaces for housing purposes poses some specific problems regarding the set up and effectiveness of transformative actions. But through this case study we have been able to verify that only through collaboration, invitation and possibility to act, is it also possible to give these spaces a certain sense of dignity, triggering new visions of change and progress in the daily temporariness of the functions carried out in these spaces.

We run the risk of not being able to significantly influence certain marginalising mechanisms of housing that trace back to the very policies on housing itself. These mechanisms prove fossilised, but it is only thanks to this collaborative method of action that we have been able to experience these mechanisms, understand them and experiment with new, more democratic and inclusive housing strategies. Moreover, the experience is not limited to the specific case in point. Within a "research through design"[12] perspective, action highlights some elements of focus which, when linked to as many reports of similar experiences in other contexts, allow us to constantly return to discussing and updating the methods and aims of research on processes to humanise housing areas for the homeless and to promote a policy of this transformation that is both necessary and possible.

ENDNOTES:

1 Gianfranco Marrone, *Corpi sociali. Processi comunicativi e semiotica del testo* (Torino: Einaudi, 2001), 323. Translated by the authors.

2 Cfr. Ibid

3 Ibid., 320. Translated by the authors.

4 According to which "much of our behaviour is cued by expectations, determined by the frames which constitute the context of action." [Daniel Miller, *Stuff* (Cambridge, UK – Malden, USA: Polity Press, 2010), chap. 2.1, ePub.]

5 Miller, chap. 2.1

6 The research "Living in the dorm" is managed by professor Cristian Campagnaro (Department of Architecture and Design of Polytechnic of Turin) and anthropologist Valentina Porcellana (Department of Philosophy and Educational Sciences of University of Turin) within the cities of Torino, Verona, Agrigento e Milano, with the patronage of fio.PSD (Italian Federation of Organis for Homeless people).

7 Cfr. Cristian Campagnaro, Valentina Porcellana, "Beauty, Participation and Inclusion," in *Art and Intercultural Dialogue. Comparative and International Education (A Diversity of Voices)* ed. Susana Gonçalves, Suzanne Majhanovich (Rotterdam: SensePublishers, 2016), 217-31

8 Michel Foucault states that heterotopias are: "real places— places that do exist and that are formed in the very founding of society— which are something like counter-sites, a kind of effectively enacted utopia in which the real sites, all the other real sites that can be found within the culture, are simultaneously represented, contested, and inverted. Places of this kind are outside of all places, even though it may be possible to indicate their location in reality. […]In the so-called primitive societies, there is a certain form of heterotopia that I would call crisis heterotopias, i.e., there are privileged or sacred or forbidden places, reserved for individuals who are, in relation to society and to the human environment in which they live, in a state of crisis […] These heterotopias of crisis [in our society] are disappearing today and are being replaced, I believe, by what we might call heterotopias of deviation: those in which individuals whose behavior is deviant in relation to the required mean or norm are placed" (Michel Foucault, "Of Other Spaces," trans. Jay Miskowiec, *Diacritics 16*, No. 1 (Spring 1986): 22-27).

9 Agamben states that "what has been banned is delivered over to its own separateness and, at the same time, consigned to the mercy of the one who abandons it - at once excluded and included, removed and at the same time captured" [Giorgio Agamben, *Homo Sacer. Sovereign Power and Bare Life*, trans. Daniel Heller-Roazen (Stanford: Stanford University Press, 1998), 109-10]. been evacuated to a secure, inland evacuation center at the time the storm event reaches the coast.

10 Cfr. Mauro Van Aken, "Introduzione," in *Antropologia: Annuario 5*, No. 5 (Roma: Meltemi, 2005): 5-13.

11 "Cantiere" in English means "construction site".

12 Cfr. Wolfgang Jonas, "Design Research and its Meaning to the Methodological Development of the Discipline", in *Design Research Now. Board of International Research in Design*, ed. Ralf Michel (Basel: Birkhäuser, 2007), 187-206.

BEING ARCHITECTURE AND ACTION

FROM DESCARTES TO FOUCAULT

by BARBARA STEHLE

The possibility to create a better world with the help of architecture is a question we all have asked ourselves in the course of our architecture studies. For the modernists among us, the topic has been a central one. From idealistic utopian projects to the pragmatic desire to design out crime in our dysfunctional environments, architects and urbanists alike have devoted hours on elaborating architectural programs to create or transform societies.

Bringing change to our human predicament has implied in various ways spatial occupations. We have used architecture commonly to occupy territory, to protect ourselves from the elements, to dwell, and to create societies. Humanity's existence and social establishment have been intrinsically linked to architecture. Our relationship with architecture is relevant to our being in the world. It exists on the ontological level.

If architecture relates to our being, it must also relate to our ways of being, and express our ethical position. Architecture is a thing that has the particularity to create a space related to who we are as a society and a people, a space reflecting our ethos and its transformations. This space would be the ground for an architectural action led by the users, with or without the help of designers, against the ills of a governing body.

Being and Architecture

René Descartes' "I think, therefore I am" is the common man's initial introduction to philosophy. However you turn it around, there is nothing left to doubt. It justifies our existence by thought outside of any incarnation. It separates our being in the world from being. What interested me in Heidegger's ontological reflection is that he was taking into account the space we exist in. His "Dasein," "Being-there" or "being in the world," refers to the experience of being that is particular to human beings. As human beings, he notes, we are dwelling on earth. We are located. And a GPS could find us. We are fundamentally bound to the space that we inhabit.[1] And to inhabit it we need architecture, we need a dwelling.

Martin Heidegger proposed something close to: I am there, thus I dwell. It is part of the defining occupations of our human condition. Something we cannot yet eliminate. Heidegger underlines the dependency "Dasein" has to time and place. He points to our need for architecture in the context of spatio-temporal existence. Much more pragmatic than Descartes, he inscribes our experience as human beings in the world and not in the mind. His "Dasein" is not a candidate for eternal life; its trajectory is completed in death.

Descartes' proposition offers possibilities of a continuum of the self beyond the extinction of the body. The French philosopher must be loved in Silicon Valley or wherever scientists are trying to remove us from localization and dependency on physical matter. And so they hope that the relevance of Heidegger's "Dasein" will soon be a thing of the past. Until then, the philosopher is useful for understanding our ontological dependency to architecture. Heidegger's position establishes an intimacy between our state of being and our dwelling places.

The nature of architecture and its relationship to the human condition comes further to light by reading Hannah Arendt.

MARTIN HEIDEGGER

HANNAH ARENDT

EYAL WEIZMAN

GEORGES-EUGÈNE HAUSSMANN

Hannah Arendt analyzed our occupations as human beings and proposed an original distinction between labor and work, inspired by her understanding of John Locke.

Arendt remarks that labor consists of "occupations (…) undertaken not for their own sake but in order to provide for the necessities of life."[2] She quotes Locke contrasting "The labor of our bodies as opposed to the work of our hands." [3] What is pointed out here are occupations meant for survival as opposed to those considered freed from necessity. Work is a creative production which leaves traces in the world, while the fruit of our labor is consumed and tends to disappear. Labor responds to the needs of our bodies, work is produced by our own will and desires.

Architecture as a human occupation has aspects of both labor and work. It is the work of one's body and one's hands. Along with the making of food and clothing it is a labor, a necessity for our survival. On the other hand, Architecture leaves endurable traces in the world. It is one of the longest lasting human creations. As an art form, architecture is distinct from the others as the only one that answers a basic life necessity. It is utilitarian and will often outlive us.

Architecture occupies a particular place at the threshold of labor and work. It is one and the other. Architecture is at once the territory of our survival and the territory of our creation. Our human condition is indexed on it in a fundamental way. Both Heidegger and Arendt's reflection offer a possible understanding of the unique part it plays in relationship to our beings. Architecture can be understood as an ontological practice, a practice of being (labor) and becoming (work).

Arendt considers a third kind of occupation: action. "Action is the political activity par excellence." [4] Actions are told to recount the story of our lives and to write our history.

"That every individual life between birth and death can eventually be told as a story with beginning and end is the pre-political and pre-historical condition of history, the great story without beginning and end. But the reason why *each human life* tells its story and why *history ultimately* becomes the storybook of mankind, with many actors and speakers and yet without any tangible authors *is that both are the outcome of action*." [5]

An architectural action would thus stem out of architecture's ontological link to our human existence. It would be an expression of necessity, creativity and the desire to give a narrative to one's life. From the political mission to the most recluse life, each expresses itself in actions. Action defines the existential modes of our beings and the way we are vis-a-vis the world. Action is in relation. It is an activity at the root of social and political expression.

For Arendt, action and speech establish our identities. Actions and speeches distinguish men amongst themselves: "They are the modes in which human beings appear to each other, not indeed as physical objects, but qua men." [6] They are the modes we use to define ourselves. They are ways in which we project ourselves in the world. They are modes of resistance and insistence. Action and speech express who we are as social and political beings. They push our stories to contribute to histories. As conveyers of our action and speech, art and architecture are historical instruments. Art and architecture contribute to each of our stories as they contribute to the history of our nations.

Politics of Space

Architecture takes over space, an aggressive quality, and offers protection, a defensive quality. Architecture is a dream military and political instrument: it is by nature defensive and can be positioned strategically. Dressed in a military way or disguised as civilian, architecture can be included in any military plan of occupation, resistance or attack. In many contexts, urban planners and architects are political strategists. Whether in war zone or not, architecture occupies space politically.

The history of architecture's association with political and military power includes the fortress, the pilgrim's cabin, as much as the portable tent. Looking for a stronghold, a definition of territory or mobility, architecture is the instrument of necessity in territorial invasion and conflicts. Politics of space like colonization and urban defense, but also social and political measures for population control, have all relied on an architectural plan. Space distribution has the greatest political and social influence. It creates hierarchy or equality, allows for freedom or restricts our movements and actions.

Theorist and architect Eyal Weizmann evokes the central role played by building and circulation strategies in territorial divisions in Israel/Palestine: "Space becomes the material embodiment of a matrix of forces, manifested across the landscape in the construction of roads, hilltop settlements, development towns and garden suburbs."[7] Architects and planners participate in the political plans made for territorial occupation. The program of these architectural developments and their consequences exemplifies the designer's political responsibility. It also shines light on the role played by civilians to put the plans into action.

Organizing the repartition of space has been one of the essential elements of social and political expression. Architectural ordering capacity participates in the establishment of urban logic and clarity. Many aspects of the design of the urban fabric contribute to the legibility of the city and to the fluidity of its functioning. The iconography of façades evokes the official order of things and the city maze offers approved circulation patterns.

Baron Haussmann's beautifying and modernizing plan for Paris in the XIX century was conceived as a

LE CORBUSIER

ROLAND BARTHES

political intervention. The renovations would bring a new social order to the city. The governmental urban reflection involved military input and hygienic modernizing spirit. One of the goals was to design out crime and minimize the possibility of revolutions. It also aimed at reducing the spread of epidemics and at creating more green spaces with new parks and gardens.

In terms of policing, Haussmann and Napoleon III included in their Parisian project a number of measures. Only to name a few: plans were to destroy medieval Parisian neighborhoods considered nests of social upheavals. They replaced small dark streets with well-lit avenues, easy to control with a cavalry. New buildings were conceived to break the concentration of a specific economical group and divide the population. Each floor of a building would host a different social segment. As you ascended, apartments were to be occupied by people from an increasingly lower social class. The goal was for the Bourgeois and aristocrats located on the lower floors to control the going and coming of the poor living on the top floors. The wealthy would be able to tell on the action of the working class. That this surveillance system ever worked is another story and points to the agency of civilians.

Rather than seeing architecture as an instrument to reinforce a hierarchical order, modernists saw it as a tool to correct social imbalance. The idea that architecture

and urban planning can improve our lives was one of the main topics of the modernist project. Good design was understood as a tool to combat the ills of our societies. Utopian and rationalist projects alike looked for solutions. Architecture could provide a new equilibrium and take down social tensions. A political agenda was never far from such projects.

Le Corbusier's title "Architecture or Revolution" exposes how his vision of architecture could prevent social unrest. Positive social change would come by improving living standards. Le Corbusier believed his architecture would diminish the need for policing and population control. A dwelling bringing greater satisfaction to the inhabitant, was the greatest tool to avoid revolutions. Happy inhabitants would be easier to govern and make peaceful citizens. It is hard not to react to the somewhat paternalistic aspect of the project. But his good intentions are clear.

Le Corbusier's concept of a machine for living aimed at defining a territory (a house) to facilitate a comfortable, efficient and hygienic lifestyle. He hoped that the machine would be used conscientiously to create better living. After the First World War, and again after the second, architects and planners dreamt of contributing to the making of a positive territory.

Each building establishes a territoriality characterized by a certain ethos. That ethos is the fruit of the personal perspective of the user and the influence of his environment. Ethos tells us about "the characteristic spirit of a culture, era, or community as manifested in its beliefs and aspirations."[8] Architecture translates the ethos of a culture in its fabric. Spaces reflect beliefs and attachments to a certain etiquette or code of ethics. They are inclusive or exclusive. They make segregation possible and communal living an option.

Deleuze and Guatari prefer the word Milieu to environment as it insists on the social and biological aspect of the surrounding. They observed that: "A building is formed in a milieu, but it also has a milieu within and around it, where new concepts and new ways of living can be shaped."[9] Nothing is stuck. The milieu is ground for transformation, hybrid solution or elimination. Possibilities abound.

As much as buildings and urban spaces express the principles of living in a particular milieu, their ethos can be practiced in opposition or in accordance to it. Forces and impulses of divergent sources have a liberating effect. The plurality of actions is always fertile ground for new programs. Buildings end up being defined by the stories they host, rather than the ones they were programmed for. Their events come out of the user's decisions. Different people at different times will take over the space, bring in their own ethos and push for different outcomes.

Creativity, Authorship and Deontology of the User

Architecture and politics are implicated in each other insofar as the users are participating and work to produce the goal expected. Users will either follow the user's manual or adapt and reuse the space in the ways they desire. Their actions will define the stories associated with these spaces. The creative user will inscribe stories in all spaces they practice. Their own invention and imagination will allow for a reinterpretation of the space. The role played by the space will be as influential as in any fictional setting.

Michel de Certeau thinks of stories as spatial trajectories. Stories are made of things, actions and events, which take place in space. Their development travels a particular territoriality. Each text is attached to a spatial context.

More than ever, Roland Barthes comes to mind. His famous, death of the author giving place to the birth of the reader, is incredibly concrete in the case of architecture. The architect cannot control the way his building will be interpreted. The architectural fabric is always something that can be transformed and instrumentalized to new ends. The final words will be in the hands of the users; New choreographies of space will emerge, new ethos, new missions. Most architectures are intervened on, reinvented and appropriated. Buildings and spaces are collectively authored by successive users and designers.

Adaptive reuse demonstrates that the initial

purpose of an architecture can be reformulated. Something of the original authorship will perhaps remain, but the architectural events and actions will be defined overwhelmingly by the people actively practicing the space. Architecture goes beyond individual authorship, it pulls in a plurality of agencies and the possibilities for multiple events. "Plurality is the condition of human"[10] underlines Arendt. The architectural condition reflects this plural state.

Nothing can be fully imposed on the multiple users. The users are only responsible for choosing their ethos and exercising their own principles. All is possible. There may be contradiction, opposition, or compliance. For those engaged in defending social liberties and willing to resist oppressive order, architecture and the urban fabric are territories open to practice.

The success of a design intervention to resist, break away from the status quo and liberate will depend on the active participation of the users. The project itself can never be the guarantee of freedom. Only the users' work and exercise of freedom can fight to preserve it.

Asked if he saw "any particular architectural projects, either in the past or the present, as forces of liberation or resistance,"[11] Michel Foucault answered:

"I do not think that it is possible to say that one thing is of the order of "liberation" and another is of the order of "oppression." (...) no matter how terrifying a given system may be, there always remain the possibilities of resistance, disobedience and oppositional groupings. On the other hand, I do not think that there is anything that is functionally- by its very nature- absolutely liberating. Liberty is a practice."[12]

Things cannot secure freedom. Beings are the only agents of that freedom.

"So there may, in fact always be a certain number of projects whose aim is to modify some constraints, to loosen, or even to break them, but none of these projects can, simply by its nature assure that people will have liberty automatically(...)"[13]

Foucault continues: "I think it is somewhat arbitrary to try to dissociate the effective practice of freedom by people, the practice of social relations, and the spatial distributions in which they find themselves. If they are separated, they become impossible to understand. Each can only be understood through the other."[14]

There is interdependency between the practice of freedom, the people's ethos, and the distribution and use of space. This is what architects have perceived and this is why they attempted to develop projects that would accompany our pursuit of liberty. But these projects and the utopian modernist machines for better living can not function independently from the strong commitment of a people.

Foucault warns against the possible corruption and diversion of well-intended machines for freedom: "Men have dreamt of liberating machines. But there are no machines of freedom, by definition. That is not to say that the exercise of freedom is completely indifferent to spatial distribution, but it can only function when there is a certain convergence; in the case of divergence or distortion it immediately becomes the opposite of that which has been intended." [15]

There can be no machine for freedom as freedom is an individual practice, not a tool.

It is easy to turn any simple meditative room into a torture chamber, or open the sky of a cell to create a soothing well of light. Any space can be re/interpreted negatively or positively. The laws and the judiciary system are abstract components that help structure the liberties of our societies. But concretely, the respect for liberty manifests itself in space through each individual. A deontological attitude from each of the space users will determine the outcome. An architectural action is always possible. It takes fierce determination and active participation. Architecture and the urban fabric are the territories of revolution, resistance and transformations. It is up to us to activate it.

ENDNOTES:

1 Martin Heidegger, "Building Dwelling Thinking" from *Poetry, Language, Thought,* translated by Albert Hofstadter, (New York: Harper Colophon Books, 1971)

2 Hannah Arendt, *The Human Condition,* (Chicago: University of Chicago Press, 1998), 83.

3 John Locke, *Second Treatise of Civil Government*, sec. 26. quoted by Arendt, *The Human Condition*, 79.

4 Arendt, 9.

5 Ibid, 184. My emphasis.

6 Ibid, 176.

7 Eyal Weizman, *A Civilian Occupation*, (Verso, 2003). 19.

8 Merriam- Webster Dictionary.

9 Andrew Ballantyne, *Deleuze and Guatari for Architects*, (Verso, 2003). 19.

10 Arendt, 8.

11 K. Michael Hays, in "Michel Foucault Space Knowledge and Power (Interview with Paul Rabinowitz)," *Architecture theory since 1968,* (Cambridge, MIT Press, 2000), 433.

12 Ibid.

13 Hays, 433.

14 Hays, 434.

15 Ibid.

Shamsia Hassani, *Dream Graffiti*, 2015

APPROPRIATING ARCHITECTURE

DIGITAL GRAFFITI AS TEMPORARY SPATIAL INTERVENTION

by DOROTHÉE KING

Introduction

In the classic first essay on the importance of graffiti in the 1970s in New York City, Norman Mailer tells us the joke about the importance of a mediated visual reality. Two Jewish grandmothers are meeting on a street. The first one is pushing a stroller: "Oh," says the other, "what a beautiful grandchild you have." "That's nothing," says the first, reaching for her pocketbook, "Wait'll I show you her picture." [1]

We might not fully notice what we directly and sensually perceive in reality – yet we react very strongly to a mediated visual reality. Graffiti artists use this knowledge to display messages they do not want to be unconsciously, but consciously acknowledged. Playing with size, colors, and remarkable calligraphy, graffiti artists publicly apply layers of mediated visual realities with the hope to provoke real change in society. Graffiti developed as a cultural technique, cheap and available to the suppressed, to react to political and social constraints. Until now most graffiti artists use their publically visible imagery to protest against authority, inequality, racism, supremacy, or ignorance. Graffiti is a tool of intervention. It comments on and criticizes existing cultural parameters.

The change-provoking, reality-mediating aspects are also true of digital graffiti. [2] Yet there are differences, which digital graffiti manifests in its temporality and its material. Digital graffiti is ephemeral in a way which physical graffiti is not. Messages are displayed temporarily. In traditional graffiti, information is scratched, scribbled, painted or sprayed on all kinds of mostly publicly visible surfaces, with the intention that the graffiti would be there for a long duration of time (if not forever). In digital graffiti the protest is no longer permanently applied to architecture. Graffiti in the form of digital images of writing, calligraphy, drawing, or paintings is temporarily projected onto facades of buildings or other visible parts of constructions. While traditional graffiti might be associated with long-term vandalism and its messages might go out of fashion quickly, digital graffiti has the advantage of being removable and can be updated. Its other notable characteristic is its digital materiality in relation to the digitalization of our environment. Digital media makes us relate differently to space; Pictures, video, and sound are portable information, available at all times, embedded in carry-on every-day-gadgets and mobile phones. As the architect Anastasia Karandinou notes in her research on ephemeral qualities of architecture, "the traditional binary opposition between the sensuous and the digital is being currently reversed." [3] We have come to a point where technology does not only change the way we interact virtually, but also alters the physical architecture surrounding us. This seems to be the next logical step: to picture digital imagery from carry-on gadgets, projecting them in greater size and thus making them publically visible interventions. With digital graffiti, we may mediate our visual environment digitally.

Some examples may serve to demonstrate the potential of digital graffiti as a form of intervention, and also show cultural differences in community engagement, mediation, and aesthetics within the realm of digital graffiti. First, I shall look at political initiatives that use digital graffiti professionally to formulate broader political statements. These initiatives choose distinct architecture to appropriate, linking the 'projection screen' with their messages, and appealing to the viewers to imagine change. Secondly, as an example for a digital graffiti community project, I will discuss 'Calligraffiti', which includes Berlin-based refugees from the Arabic world. This community project links to the politics and aesthetics of graffiti that showed up during the Arab spring, and at the same time relates to the Arabic cultural tool to concatenate written words or calligraphy with the facades of public buildings. Thirdly, I will show the work of the Afghani graffiti artist Shamsia Hassani, who uses digital graffiti in the form of photo-shop projects, applying colorful and peaceful elements to heal the broken architecture and communities in her war-ridden home country.

Digital Grafitti

In 2014 the environmentalist group Greenpeace projected the message 'Listen to the People, Not the Polluters' on the United Nations building in New York City, shortly

after hundreds of thousands of people demonstrated on the streets to demand climate action. The projection was later translated into different languages and was shared instantly in digital media with communities around the world, who also held marches and protests drawing attention to climate change on the same weekend.[4] Through using the UN building as projection screen, Greenpeace literally appealed to the nations to unite, addressing global responsibility for climate control. Another example is Greenpeace's 'Planet Earth First' digital graffiti campaign seen 2017 in Hamburg and the Vatican, following the US president's travel to the G20 summit and a meeting with the Pope.

On Women's Day March 8, 2017, the feminist activist group Team Vulvarella projected two huge images of a naked woman with a face mask on the façade of the US Embassy in Berlin. Deliberately choosing time and place, the activists protested against sexual harassment and the US travel ban against citizens of several countries in the Middle East.

In both cases the projection screens are chosen upon the basis of a calculation. The message to be spread is linked to the place which represents its cause. Digital graffiti is addressing the pedestrians walking by, and additionally the larger institutions, whose facades are used for the projections. Also, the graffiti acts digitally in two ways: Firstly, through the technique of digital projection, and secondly, through the massive viral impact on digital media that follows the actual projection event.

Digital Calligraffiti

During the Arab spring graffiti was an often-used tool to formulate visible protest against political oppression. Graffiti was seen in such diverse forms as fast scribbling, slogans, and scenic murals.[5] Voices that were silenced or whitewashed become louder through recurring graffiti.[6] One special form of this graffiti is Calligraffiti. Looking back to a 1400-year-old Muslim aniconic culture of emphasizing the depiction of words over the representation of animated beings, it appears to be a logical step to combine traditional calligraphy with graffiti. Another twist is applied by projecting calligraphy as digital graffiti.

In the Summer of 2017, the Berlin based Public Art Lab, a platform for urban art projects, organized a project with migrants from Syria, Afghanistan, Iraq, Senegal, and other countries.[7] The main idea was to transform the urban environment into projection screens and communication platforms. Subway stations and public building interiors and exteriors served as boards for calligraphic messages. The projection tool was a simple live projector named 'Infl3ctor', developed by the artists Michael Ang and Hamza Abu Ayyash.[8] The messages spread were written primarily in Arabic and German. Calls were made for love, art, and peace. Yet also more concrete political messages were spread, such as "It's

Shamsia Hassani, *Dream Graffiti*, **2015**
Copyright: Shamsia Hassani

amazing to take pictures in the street without being stopped by police."[9]

In this case of digital graffiti, the messages and the aesthetics of the digital graffiti are an important factor in the acknowledgment of the cultural heritage of the new Berliners. Calligraffiti serves as a community builder. Through appropriating public space, one belongs to a community. This is true for digital graffiti in 2017, as it was true for graffiti in 1972, when Hugo Martinez, who organized the first graffiti association, stated that "graffiti writing is a way of gaining status in a society where to own property is a way to have an identity."[10]

Digital Dreaming Graffiti

Shamsia Hassani is a famous graffiti artist in Kabul. Being a professor of Sculpture at Kabul University, she has brought street art to the center of her home town. She uses colorful graffiti to cover up the negative reminders of the war on real architecture and also in the minds of the people. She claims that "image has more effect than words, and it's a friendly way to fight."[11] Shamsia Hassani also presents her ideas digitally. Her project 'Dreaming Graffiti' is a series of photo-shopped images. She paints and decorates war-ruins from Kabul and shares these images online. She imagines a different environment through interacting virtually with the physical architecture surrounding her. Though this sub-category of digital graffiti may not be tangible in the physical space, it has the power to change the way in which the community sees the potential of its environment.

Conclusion

Is digital graffiti the new tool for the generation of digital natives to resist, protest, and engage? With the examples above we see that going digital allows a "displacement and assemblage of space,"[12] and leads to a re-organizing of the aesthetics of architecture with all its symbols and power structures. Digital graffiti is a powerful tool for protest and intervention. And the practical advantages of digital graffiti over traditional graffiti are obvious. One does not have to get close to the architecture onto which one intends to project. Even fenced-in buildings can be turned into a projection screen. One may even choose the building in relation to the message of the graffiti. Also, digital graffiti does not cause damage to property and is therefore not a criminal act.

We return to the joke about the picture in the pocketbook. Now is the time to get our pocketbooks – aka phones and tablets – to show our environment the real truth. This time we are not only showing our mediated reality to our friends. This time our messages are projected, are publically visible, and go viral. All one needs is some courage, maybe a good projector – but usually a flash light does the job.

ENDNOTES:

1 Norman Mailer, *The Faith of Graffiti* (Westport: Praeger Publishers,1974), ch.1.

2 There are non-protest versions of digital graffiti, such as street festivals and commercial advertisement. For this article, I want to focus on digital graffiti as interventions and political acts.

3 Anastasia Karandinou, *Theories and Practices of the Ephemeral in Architecture* (Surrey: Ashgate, 2013), preface.

4 Molly Dorozenski,''Greenpeace Delivers People's Message on Eve of Climate Summit, ''September 23, 2014. http://www.greenpeace.org/usa/greenpeace-delivers-peoples-message-eve-climate-summit/

5 Pascal Zoghbi and Don Karl aka Stone, *Arabic Graffiti*, (Berlin: From Here to Fame, 2011), 57.

6 Rana Jarbou, "The Seeds of a Graffiti Revolution," in *Walls of Freedom - Street Art of the Egyptian Revolution*" ed. by Basma Handy, Don Karl (Berlin: From Here to Fame, 2014), 9-12, 9.

7 "Digital Calligraffiti," *Public Art Lab*, accessed November 11, 2017, http://www.publicartlab-berlin.de/blog/2017/09/05/digital-calligraffiti-2/.

8" Michael Ang, Infl3ctor, Michael Ang," accessed November 11, 2017, http://www.michaelang.com/project/infl3ctor.

9 DJ Pangburg, "Activists Are Projecting Digital "Calligraffiti" Onto Walls in Berlin," accessed November 11, 2017, https://creators.vice.com/en_us/article/nz57wz/activists-are-projecting-digital-calligraffiti-onto-walls-in-berlin.

10 Norman Mailer, *The Faith of Graffiti* (Westport: Praeger Publishers,1974), ch.1

11 Shamsia Hassani, interview with auopsiart, accessed November 12, 2017, http://autopsiart.com/shamsia-hassani/.

12 Karandinou, 201.

Drury live in the subway, Berlin, 2017

Model of the proposed elephant refuge project by Kristoffer Tejlgaard

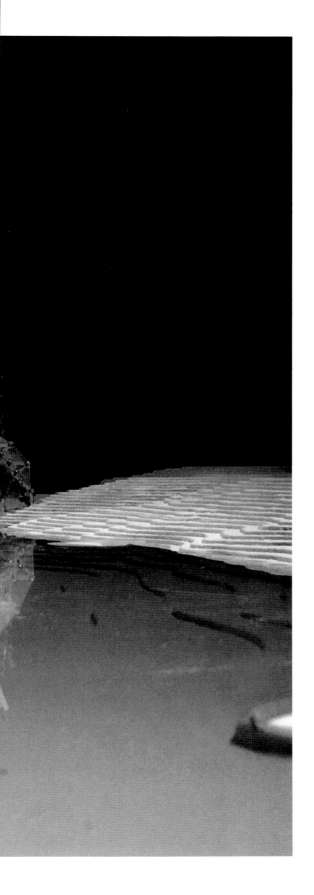

THE ELEPHANT REFUGE

'PRE-USE' VS 'RE-USE'

by HEINRICH HERMANN

The project introduced here is the culmination of an artistic vision by Daniel Peltz, evolved in phases over more than ten years around his deep reflection on the act of giving and taking refuge in our time. It was triggered in part by the recent arrival of refugees from Syria and Afghanistan in Rejmyre, Sweden, where his research was focused. He also began to reflect on the unemployed in the advanced economies of Europe, including Sweden, and on startling parallels to the lot of teak wood-harvesting elephants in Myanmar, recently having become unemployed due to over-harvesting. He chose to explore 'the practice of giving and taking refuge' by way of, conceptually, accommodating unemployed elephants from Myanmar in Rejmyre, Sweden.

Peltz commissioned the Danish architect Kristoffer Tejlgaard to design that refuge, in close consultation with him. His thinking had evolved into one of understanding the act of building refuge itself as the core of his vision, independent from the elephants' actual arrival at, and use of, the refuge designed for their very needs. He sees the project as a built meditation on the act of giving and taking shelter.

Peltz states, "I refer to the model I am working with as 'adaptive pre-use,' wherein a structure is designed and built, by a specific community for a specific, incongruous purpose, that it will never serve. The community builds the structure and then is left with the task of how

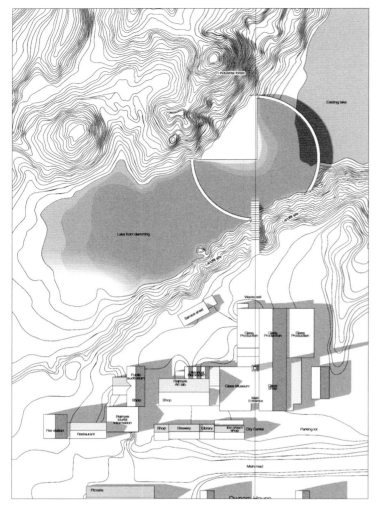

The Project

Tejlgaard's design takes place at the intersection of a location-specific artistic vision and a number of socio-economic, environmental, and other issues that find synthesis in using and re-using parts of the expansive site behind the glass factory with its brook and forest beyond.

From its beginnings, Rejmyre had been organized along the northwest to southeast-running street now called Glasbrucksvägen. The original factory owner's residence was built south of the street, set back and flanked by two buildings across a shared park-like green space. From the owner's residence a footpath extended axially across the street to the factory's main entrance and continued right through the tall smokestack, which has been Rejmyre's most visible marker ever since. At the northeastern end of the factory and axially aligned with the smoke stack, the glassmaking refuse left the building through a large gate and was dumped into the valley beyond. Today the main complex comprises on the street side the glass museum left of the entrance recess and the glass shop to its right, while the glass production extends across the entire rear volume, starting roughly beyond the smoke stack.

After first closely studying Rejmyre, its glass factory, its production history and the site's topography, altered and narrowed by two centuries of dumping the factory's refuse, Tejlgaard's proposal, commissioned by Peltz, is as follows:

Paramount above all was to design the elephant refuge so they and their care takers are accommodated in the best possible ways. Among others, elephants need water, a forest, and long vistas – all pointing to the currently severely polluted land beyond the factory that straddles the brook that feeds a small lake further northeast. Thus, they chose the area that also leads into an expansive forest to its north. They think of the elephant refuge as symbolizing the future of Rejmyre's development but want to intimately link it, as the town's natural further growth, with older Rejmyre.

Tejlgaard accordingly situates its geometry and organization in alignment with the historic development axis from the former factory owner's residence across the street to the factory's entry portal, through the smoke stack, and its rear opening. His first gesture was to mark with a large circle the intersection of the brook with the view axis from the rear gate and smoke stack. Within this circle would be the elephants' and their keepers' living area, their swimming area, and the beginnings of the forest beyond.

To accomplish all this, he conceived of the circle as a cylinder whose walls dam the brook uphill and straddle land and water for the elephants to swim in, co-planar with the new pond upstream and overlooking the valley below. The circular area comfortably houses the elephant refuge and is covered and thermally protected

to repurpose this purpose-built new structure. It has an element of the illogical but is more properly grounded in seeking strategies to provoke the possible in places that have been abandoned [in the anthropologist Anna L. Tsing's words 'seeking life in the ruins of capitalism's abandoned asset fields']. This is done through the act of building, as an embodied, dialogic process, and through the act of considering the needs of an unknown other as a way of thinking the act of giving and taking refuge. In the specific case of the glass factory town of Rejmyre, we are designing and planning to build a refuge for elephants who are unemployed from the teak logging industry in Myanmar. "

Both Peltz's vision and Tejlgaard's subsequent design for a group of elephants and their keepers - carried out to very exacting specifications even though neither of them are intended to arrive, and hence will require adaptation to a new use right after completion - pose the question of how to properly categorize a work such as this.

The proposed site plan for the elephant refuge and its relationship to the glass factory

by a greenhouse of mostly transparent skin spanning a structural web of wood and steel. The elephants would be able to swim to the dam's inner edge, with unimpeded long vistas both uphill, downhill, and into the woods, as well as towards the glass factory anchored by its smokestack. The top of the circle would be just a little higher than the water level and walkable for the keepers inside the glazing. On the outside, a shallow passage might allow local people coming from the town center to walk to the forest beyond. For all who are admitted to this passage, the afforded long vistas and the unique play of light and shadows cast by the greenhouse's skin would be equally enjoyable, as would be the dematerializing aspects of the water, both in the lake below, in the elephants' swimming area, and the upstream pond beyond.

Peltz commissioned Tejlgaard due to an admiration for his Domes of Vision in Stockholm and Copenhagen, both built as a continuous structural web of wood and steel, covered in polycarbonate sheets, resting on a perimeter ring on the ground. Tejlgaard felt such a dome shape was not appropriate here. Instead he proposed a structural system akin to his domes of vision but here suspended from three outward leaning teepee-like structural towers at the circle's perimeter and three large structural arches spanning between them. He firmly anchors the web to the ground in the short zones behind the three towers, which will be made of heavy timber stems and thus relate well to the woods beyond. These towers will also serve to vent the interior and in their upper reaches house the mahouts, the elephants' caretakers. Below the structural arches, which follow the circular plan geometry of the dam, glazed walls provide a warm interior for the elephants while allowing them to visually experience the environment beyond and feel connected with it. Tejlgaard wants to also grow the food for the elephants year-round in portions of it. In addition, it will house all areas needed for the proper care of the animals, their medical checkups, etc.

Environmental pollution as opportunity

The selected refuge site happens also to be the most polluted area and fortunately the Swedish government has set aside the needed funds for cleaning up the environmental harm caused over two centuries by the glass factory. Peltz and Tejlgaard see a great opportunity in these funds and propose a win-win scenario for Rejmyre, its environmental health, and a unique link to the history of glass-making here. They propose to have the environmental cleanup operation not carried out by a far-away company but instead by the citizens of Rejmyre, many of whom are after all the descendants of those workers who in the past centuries had to do the polluting on the factory's behalf. The income from the cleanup funds would thus flow into Rejmyre's economy and revitalize it.

But Peltz and Tejlgaard's thinking goes further than the economic level. They want all the layers of glass discarded over 200 years to be melted into multi-colored glass bricks. They can then be used for building both the visible portions of the dam as well as the path and flight of stairs that link the refuge with the factory and form an important new second entrance to the complex. This material metamorphosis, a genuine adaptive reuse of the waste into magnificently mysterious multi-colored building blocks spread over the once severely polluted area in a healing new order, would be a dignified witness to the town's historic past.

Incorporating the path from the factory down to the sanctuary into the forest, would provide for new life, and would turn a backside not ever to be seen into a wonderful realm to be discovered. In the reverse direction, one could now enter the factory and Rejmyre, after being inspired by a new and different way of knowing about its place and history within the larger region. At a minimum, the presence of this complex would make Rejmyre a magnet for visitors and benefit local businesses. But it may actually serve as a catalyst for businesses and others to settle there and bring about as of yet unimaginable positive change. The reuse of the factory's glass refuse to cast glass bricks for key portions of the refuge and its physical connection with the factory would be transformative for Rejmyre's identity and bring its history alive.

'PRE-USE' vs 'RE-USE'

Peltz conceived of the refuge from early on as a physical complex that would only accommodate the elephants conceptually. He characterizes as 'adaptive pre-use' the design he asked Tejlgaard to create, as it would require adaptation for an unknown subsequent use by the community. His artistic vision is certainly driven by an honorable underlying motivation. The refuge as introduced is actually a clear case of adaptive reuse, in the form of an addition to an existing factory site, while serving an entirely new purpose. The existing structure's current function would be left unchanged except for minor modifications, having to do with enhancing/ making more palpable the spatial experience of moving through the glass factory, and through the former waste portal that would now give access to the new intervention.

Without any intent of bringing the elephants, the refuge de facto has only a conceptual use function but no actual one. The numerous specific features accommodating the elephants, while distinctive and intriguing, would initially be physically built empty gestures. Only after the community would identify a new purpose and spend the potentially significant resources to adapt it would it finally serve a dedicated purpose. As adaptation requires the pre-existence of an object that can be adapted - the refuge would thus be the object that

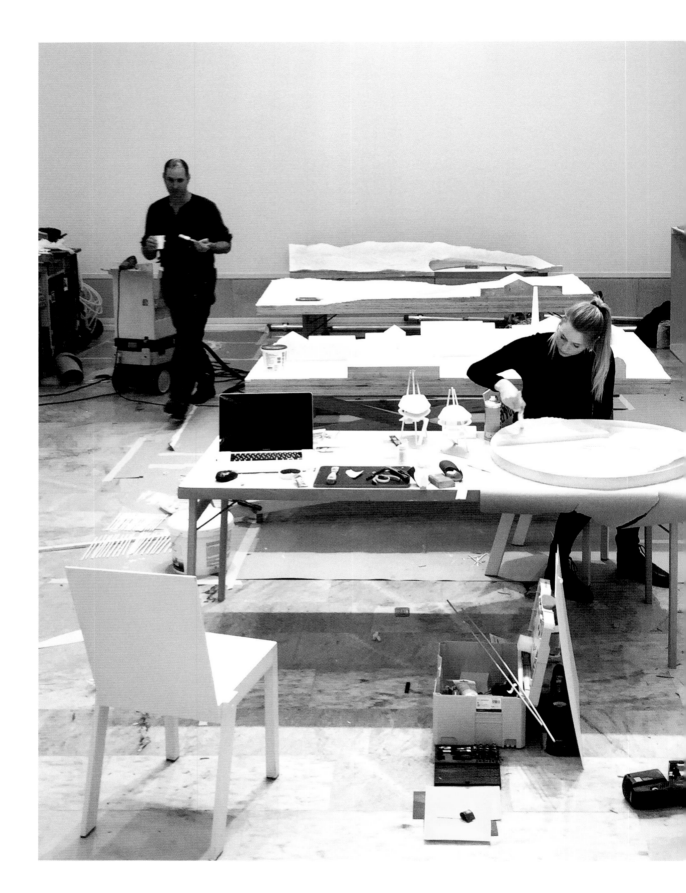

The model for the elephant refuge, in process

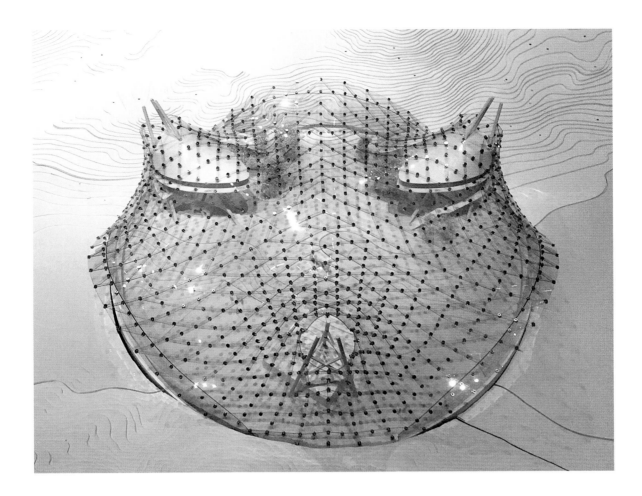

subsequently gets adapted. Therefore, one cannot talk of adaptive pre-use here either.

While acknowledging Peltz's understanding the act of building refuge itself as the core of his vision, is there a vehicle by which one attempts the same idealist pursuit that would design directly for the final use, without necessitating the subsequent adaptive reuse phase? A possible scenario for such a concept could, for example, be imagined for a future described by an Oxford University study[1] on expected drastic changes to the work-world as we now know it today. It predicted that within the short span of only 25 years, about 50% of all jobs will cease to exist in the way we know them now, resulting from accelerating mechanization, computerization, artificial intelligence, robotics, automation, and other technologies. What might be the repercussions of such massive shifts for the practice of architecture and adaptive reuse? By implication, new buildings to accommodate many categories of present-day jobs will likely be built with the anticipation that the functions they are built for now may disappear within only a few years, after which the buildings may have to undergo possibly substantial adaptations for new, only then knowable

needs. The uncertainty about rapidly changing use functions will most likely not result in custom-designing spaces to optimally meet a current use function (as was done in the refuge, even though only conceptually), but in much more generic buildings to enable a wider range of adaptability options.

In our rapidly changing world, might a concept developed for elephants that would never arrive perhaps have its purpose?

In the end, Peltz and Tejlgaard have achieved a memorable moment in refuge design. Should an adaptation to another use be required in the future, the proposed project allows for the majestic architecture to remain in its revitalizing relation to both the immediate site and the wider Town of Rejmyre.

ENDNOTES:
1 Carl Benedikt Frey and Michael A. Osborne. "The Future of Employment," Working Paper, Oxford Martin School, University of Oxford, September 17, 2013, https://www.oxfordmartin.ox.ac.uk/downloads/academic/future-of-employment.pdf (accessed Jan. 5, 2018).

The roof of the proposed elephant refuge

UNDER THE RADAR

JOE GARLICK ON REAL ESTATE DEVELOPMENT AND EQUITY

by ELIZABETH DEBS AND LILIANE WONG

Often unseen and unheralded, an active industry of community based organizations works to revitalize marginalized communities throughout the United States. Community development corporations (CDCs) are major providers of affordable housing and, more significantly, build support for the intangible well being of the community through initiatives specifically tailored to local needs. It can be easy to wonder at the challenging state of the world today and it is therefore especially heartening to hear about the multitude of ways that positive change is steadily being made under the radar.

Working with residents, businesses, and partner institutions to enrich neighborhood life and make affordable housing opportunities available throughout, Northern Rhode Island NeighborWorks Blackstone River Valley (NWBRV) has been active in the region since 1987. Woonsocket, where NWBVR has its origins, is the 6th largest city in Rhode Island, with a population of 41,000. It is an ethnically diverse low-income community in which a quarter of the residents live below the poverty line. While owning a home is a marker for household prosperity, in Woonsocket the homeownership rate is only 38%, 25% below the national average.[1]

Joe Garlick is celebrating his 24th year as Executive Director of NWBRV. During his tenure, they have created over 500+ units of affordable housing, including 350+ rental units and an additional 150+ home ownership opportunities.

NWBRV's real estate portfolio, worth $100 million, includes projects of different scales and typologies, from

An historic mill building along the Blackstone River in Woonsocket slated for future conversion to residential units

single family homes to commercial development and the arts: ClockTower Apartments, a conversion of an historic mill; Constitution Hill, renovated historic homes; The Meadows, an affordable development for people older than 62. This work is recognized through numerous awards from Outstanding Smart Growth Leader Award to Special Congressional Recognition and Historical Preservation & Heritage Commissions' Awards.

Joe Garlick is not part of the List of Famous Real Estate Developers that includes Stephen Ross, Sheldon Adelson and Donald Trump (ranked number 45). He shares his thoughts with Int|AR about his life's work, work that constitutes acts of generosity within the communities of Rhode Island.

You have spent much of your career working with the communities of Northern Rhode Island: first, in the Woonsocket City Planning Department, then as part of four RI CDCs and, since 1994, as the Executive Director of NWBRV. What inspired you to follow this path?

JG: Several things over the course of my early life contributed to this path. In a Pawtucket elementary school during the 60s, I was taught by a nun who was really interested in the civil rights movement. As she always talked about it in class, she planted a seed for civil rights and equity. Later, at the start of my master's program, I went on a field trip to a CDC in Jersey City, one that was involved in a neighborhood plan. It was run by Rick Cohen, of the Council for Responsible Philanthropy. I believe he was the Planning Director of Jersey City at the time and he supported the non-profit in this neighborhood planning effort. It was captivating to see this neighborhood process where more than one hundred residents were designing a plan to deal with abandoned houses. Right there, even though I didn't know what it was as a career, I decided that this was what I wanted to do.

That career turned out to focus on real estate development but for non-profit purposes. As a community development corporation you work with a range of projects such as historic renovations, adaptive re-use, new construction, brownfields, and green technologies. How does your work differ from that of for-profit real estate developers? What defines the work of the non-profit developer?

JG: The primary vehicle today for the non-profit real estate developer is the low-income housing tax credit, which funds 60 or 70% of the cost of a rental housing project. That is the main stay of development work. With the change in administration and the change in the tax code, that market is in some turmoil. The pricing on the credit is not as good as it had been in years past. It has opened up a bigger gap for financing a project. The other 30 or 40% that needs to be raised might require 8 to 10 other different sources to fill that gap.

There is some State funding - the state of Rhode Island just passed a housing bond last year. There is funding through financial institutions, whose regulatory agencies have programs through which they participate, such as the federal Home Loan Bank of Boston. There are other federal programs: Community Development Block Grants, the Home Program. We use many sources as each project is uniquely different. Some of the financing is particular to the type of project. For example, historic deals have historic tax credits.

I don't think there are any for-profit developers in their right minds who would want to deal with the number of funding sources, the bureaucracy. When the economy gets bad, they think that non-profits have it easy and then... they get a taste of it. For-profit developers don't have the pain if they don't need to.

Has your non-profit status and the complex financing mechanisms caused you to be creative in seeking out new ways to deliver projects?

JG: One of the things we do as an organization lies in the structuring of the project to possibly expand the boundaries of the typical development. For example, in one of our early rehabilitation projects, we added home childcare units. It was an opportunity for multifamily buildings that we were renovating to include units for a home child-care business. Using finished basements, we were able to provide a little more space to take care of kids and not necessarily in the family's living space. This is an example of how we layer on resources to develop new programs. We've done some mixed-use developments where we extended the commercial/residential typology to include neighborhood commercial enterprises on the first floor, below the residential units. In our recent project, the Millrace Kitchen of Woonsocket, this commercial enterprise is a kitchen incubator to encourage neighborhood start-ups. We try to generate new lines of resources to help fill the funding gap and, in doing so, also address some new neighborhood needs as well.

Woodridge Estate uses the community housing land trust model of homeownership. Could you tell us about the concept in which land is deeded in perpetuity for affordable housing?

JG: The idea of a land trust is a national model that was piloted almost 50 years ago in the 70s and 80s by the Institute for Community Economics based in Greenfield, MA. It is based on a contract, called the Land Lease, between the homeowner and the non-profit entity that owns the land, in which one agrees to sell only to a person in a certified income bracket.

Woodridge happened in the early 2000s when prices were really slow in taking off in Rhode Island, in particular, in Woonsocket. It seemed a good strategy to get that project off the ground during the slump. One of the pitfalls was that the city did not want the project and we

THE CLOCKTOWER

CLOCKWISE FROM TOP LEFT:
Heritage Place, $10.2M conversion of a hardware facility to 43 units of housing and commercial space;
Woodridge Estates, $4.5M development of 26 affordable homes on 13 acres of land trusted property;
$15 million Stillwater Redevelopment Project, conversion of an historic mill into 47 apartments and
offices; $500,000 Art Center with artist-in-residence live/work; Covered entry stairs at Heritage Place

ended up in court. The city simply did not want afford-able housing, and this is an on going issue.

The land trust was also something they didn't under-stand. When someone moves out they can put their house on the market at market value, minus the price of the land itself. The buyer just pays for the improve-ments made to the land. At the time of the project, the Woonsocket real estate market took a dive after the foreclosure prices. When we built the houses, they sold for about $105,000-139,000. The foreclosure prices have climbed back up to about $140,000 -145,000 which is a lower but still very affordable price. The market is start-ing to take off again. One of the occupants is moving. He bought it for $100,000 and sold it for $130,000. The other houses in that area, not in the land trust, are in the $200,000 range.

What is the size of your staff? Of the full-time staff, how many are actually working on projects in real estate development?
JG: There are 15 full-time staff and another 15 who work part-time in the after-school program. There are also interns and volunteers, probably 4 or so, from AmeriCorps VISTA. 3 of us work in the real estate division.

What is an estimated value of the square footage of work that the real estate division produces?
JG: We have built about five hundred units of which there are 350+ units of rental housing and an additional 150+ affordable home ownership opportunities. In total, they are worth about $100 million dollars.

I think our readers would be very surprised to know that there is such a robust industry doing this work. Why is it not visible to the larger population?
JG: I find it amazing that anyone would not know about this sector. But I probably shouldn't be so surprised since we work in marginalized communities that people don't pay attention to anyway. How would that work be on the radar anymore so than the people who actually live there?

While real estate development is an important component of the work and finances the rest of your activities, it seems that the community engagement is more at the heart of the mission. How do you engage different groups and what do you need for equitable development? What kinds of programs do you offer in addition to the actual physical manifestation of the work?
JG: My job is finance and fundraising. The non-real estate aspect, however, is what makes it exciting to go to work everyday. That's the real stuff. The non-real estate component is what I hope the real estate transactions lead to. That is what generates income. In this part of

the process, we get a chance to be more creative, and do more interesting work in the community.

There are lots of assets in neighborhoods. But I hope we are bringing something exciting and new to communities that they never thought would exist in these places. We do this through programs such as our Creative Placemaking Initiative which grants funding to revitalize arts and culture in downtown Woonsocket. We have had various artists, writers, budding chefs who have lived in the neighborhood and produced work. Giving them the place to do such projects is definitely outside the realm of real estate development. Any money we have earned has been put back into this kind of program enrichment. It is an enrichment that addresses a different level of need in us, a little more spiritual than the basic necessity for a roof over our heads. It includes exciting ventures like the new grant we recently received for building a community bread oven in Woonsocket. I just had a meeting with the mason yesterday.

NWBRV has numerous complimentary programs that go beyond simple shelter. Can you tell us about initia-tives that focus on education and economic advance-ment such as the Homebuyer and Landlord training program ?
JG: Home ownership is one of the major asset build-ing activities we can engage in for households and families. Acknowledging the importance of homebuyer education, understanding financial capability is a model we brought to Woonsocket. Many communities of color haven't had access to that opportunity. Our Homeownership Center model is focused on provid-ing education around the home-buying process, where credit has become a barrier for accessing affordable mortgage lending products. The mortgage market meltdown of the last decade has been a living labora-tory of ' how not to do it.' The Homeownership Center is focused on helping people to qualify for those funds and to do it in a way that they're not being taken advantage of. That's the goal of our Homeownership Center and the staff there.

One of the counselors for our Self-Help Housing program, an opportunity through the US Department of Agriculture enabling you to build your own home, is trying to help minorities build houses in a fairly white suburban community. As a black woman, she has put herself out there, championing minority applicants in this white community. She has had issues to make an entree for them to both own a home and to be in a com-munity that is not a mixed one. She's very passionate about it and that is the kind of staff required to advance this type of change.

Community Development in the US has its roots in civil rights and social activism and you are doing some work today that has to do with race and place. Can you tell us more about this initiative?

JG: As an organization, we are participating in a national initiative called REDI (Race Equity Diversity Inclusion) that originated through our national organization, NeighborWorks America. As a national organization, they were interested in looking at the relevance of such issues to their work at the grassroots level. Based in DC, they coordinate resource development for the "network," as they call it, of the CDCs around the country, the 250 or so groups of which we are one in Rhode Island.

There was an incongruence between the communities where many CDCs work, which are already communities of color, while the organizations are predominantly white. They reached out and asked the organizations to participate in what might be called a soul-searching process. They convened national training sessions to sort one's views on race, equity and other issues.

The initial sessions focused on a series of relevant readings. The next level of work was to create an E team, an equity team within the organization to look at the issues as they relate to one's own organization. At NWBVR, we are at an early stage with a group of six who convene monthly to discuss both the readings and how race has impacted our work in this period. The questions are open ended but intense. One doesn't often have time to have these kinds of conversations in the context of the workday. Our work in these sectors is so outcome focused in a sense while the focus of the sessions was to determine what this work means to our organization, what it means personally. It is uncomfortable, there is no end product at least in this early stage - it's more just to figure out one's own baggage, if you will.

The thing that interested me about participating is that the housing that we do is the foundation for a more racially diverse and equitable place. Where people live is really critical to changing some of these dynamics in communities and around the country. As a small non-profit organization, we control some resources. It then becomes an issue of resource allocation and how we are doing it so as not to perpetuate inequity. As there are younger folks coming up in the ranks of our organization, it is a good place to have such a conversation.

Who is the next generation of CDC leaders? Where are they coming from, especially in the political climate we find ourselves in today?

JG: This question is making me think in a broader way about REDI, the race initiative. It's interesting to think about where the field came from and where it should go. There should be more people of color doing the work. But we are seeing them coming up through the ranks.

Engaging the kids for AmeriCorps VISTA, their service year or two, is really important because it gives them a

taste for it. It's usually a different experience too. When people come to our organization, they haven't worked in anything like it before. They either really like it or they can't stand it. Most of them really enjoy it and stay for a second year.

There is science on program evaluation and performance success measures. But how would you personally measure success? What tells you that you've done a good job either on a project, on the progress of your community as a whole, or moving the industry in a particular way?

JG: It's easy in the sector to point to the numbers of units that we build. We have x numbers of hundreds of apartments, X numbers of homeowners and so on. We keep track of that because funders want to know. So those are the easy measures of success, in some ways.

But what is the real impact on how people's lives have changed? I don't think we keep track of that well. I have individual connections in the neighborhood. I see my staff who generally live in the neighborhoods they work in. They seem to be very committed to the work and enjoy their job. That makes me feel that the people that do the work for the organization are happy and are making a difference in their community. So that to me is important.

As for personal measures, I get these projects done and it was fun doing them. I guess there's always frustration that if there was enough money you could do something better. I always like to learn how I can do it better or differently. I haven't yet found the one that tells me that now I've done it and I'm good.

We definitely make a difference with our work. Because of our work, many have a roof over their heads. They have a place where their kids can go after school. They are on track to buy their first house and build assets for their family. Now we even have people who will start a little business, you know. But there are ways .... I don't know what they are ... but I have to believe that there are ways to make people's lives even better.

FOOTNOTES:
1 Demographics from https://datausa.io/profile/geo/Woonsock-etri/, accessed 01.15.18

Location: Lisbon, Portugal

Construction Area: 2837.18m²

Date: 2016/2017

Owner:
AR.CO – CENTRO DE ARTE E COMUNICAÇÃO VISUAL

Designer:
SANTA-RITA ARQUITECTOS, João Santa-Rita

Collaborators:
Pedro Guedes Lebre; Artur Simões Dias;
Carolina Portugal; João Vidal Sousa

Structures: Teixeira Trigo, Lda; Eng. João Leite Garcia

Other Engineering and Systems:
GRAUCELCIUS,CONSULTORES DE ENGENHARIA, GESTÃO E
PLANEAMENTO, LDA, Eng. Carlos Oliveira

Construction Supervisor:
TEIXEIRA TRIGO, LDA; Eng. João Cordeiro

Contractor:
GUALDIM NUNES DA SILVA, LDA. Eng. Bruno Ribeiro

Photographer:
Inês Guedes Lebre, Nuno Martinho

SECOND ACT

CONVERSION OF THE MERCADO DE XABREGAS

by JOÃO SANTA-RITA

Dating to the mid 20th century, the Xabregas Market complex in Lisbon, Portugal, is made up of three buildings, creating the sense of an urban structure, and an atrium onto which the interior spaces of the buildings open. Despite its Modernist nature, it nonetheless exhibits a certain compromise with the past, evident in the design of its window frames and some of its open spaces.

The buildings were temporarily occupied by workshops of the Lisbon City Hall, and underwent functional adaptations that altered some of their original character - although the most relevant features, such as the space and configuration of the main building, with its undulating rooftop, or the north and south facades marked by the brise-soleil, remained.

The nature of the buildings and their spatial structure were naturally adaptable to the programs of Ar.Co, the center of Art and Visual Communications. More specifically, the spaces with strong workshop attributes will accommodate programs of drawing, painting, photography, cinema, and jewelry. On the other hand, the character and nature of the new workrooms and services found the market, with its informal character, to be an ideal space for their activities. As such, it called for a project of punctual adaptations.

The project was carried out amidst great financial restrictions and a short completion time. It was based on a cautious assessment of the type of project to be carried out, developed from the beginning to the end, always first through quantification and then design. It was a different approach for a project that required extreme safeguards of investment and execution time.

Besides the required upgrade of infrastructures to guarantee proper conditions for occupancy and functioning of the center, and the redesign of the large scale open spaces with glass, a series of interventions of an architectural nature was adopted to create a sense of identity. These interventions establish a reflective language of the current project, superimposing a new era to that of the original market. They assign new meaning while attempting to recapture its Modernist past.

PROJECT CREDITS, INFORMATION AND BIBLIOGRAPHIES

EDITORIAL

Image Credits_ Ambrogio Lorenzetti (https://commons.wikimedia. org/wiki/File:Lorenzetti ambrogio bad govern. det.jpg), „Lorenzetti ambrogio bad govern. det", marked as public domain, more details on Wikimedia Commons: https://commons.wikimedia.org/wiki/ Template:PD-old

FARAWAY, SO CLOSE

Name of the project_ FRAC Nord- Pas de Calais; Location_ Dunkirk, France; Name of design firm_ Lacaton & Vassal Architectes; Names of designers involved in project_ Anne Lacaton & Jean Philippe Vassal, Florian de Pous (chief project), Camille Gravellier (construction supervision), Yuko Ohashi; Client_ Communauté Urbaine de Dunkerque; Structural and Mechanical Engineering_ Secotrap; Metal Structure_ CESMA; Year completed_ 2013 – 2015; Cost of construction_ 12M Euros net; Website_ www.lacatonvassal. com; Name of Photographer and Image Credits_ fig. 01-05 by Philippe Ruault; fig. 06 by Florent Michel, © 11h45m.com

TEMPORARY ACTS

Interview conducted by_ Kristina Anilane and Luis Sacristan Murga; Interviewees_ Carolina Caicedo and Xavi Llarch Font; Image Credits_ courtesy of Dosfotos and The Decorators

EVERYBODY'S HOUSE

Name of project_ *The Rosa Parks House Project*; Location_ Detroit, Berlin, Providence; Name of artist_ Ryan Mendoza; Name(s) of key architects involved in project_ João José Santos & Diogo Vale; Website_ www.ryan-mendoza.com; www.whitehousefilm.net; Image Credits_ fig. 01-07, 14-15 by Liliane Wong; fig. 08, 17, 19 by Fabia Mendoza, fig. 09 by Elaine Fredrick, Courtesy of WaterFire; fig. 10-13, 16 by João José Santos & Diogo Vale; fig. 18 by Stefano Corbo; fig. 20 by Erin Cuddigan, Courtesy of WaterFire.

TACTICAL URBANISM WHERE IT MATTERS

Image Credits_ fig. 01. Help Build a Playground, by Public Workshop; fig 02. Story time in the Logan Parklet, by PhilaNOMA; fig. 03. Street games are age-old urban tactics, by Public Workshop; fig. 04. Night guardians, by Public Workshop; fig. 05. Light towers, by Sikora Wells appel/Group Melvin Design; fig. 06. Street games are age-old urban tactics, by Public Workshop; fig. 07. Night guardians, by Public Workshop; fig 08. Roosevelt Plaza Park, by Sikora Wells appel/Group Melvin Design; fig 09. The Grove, by Sikora Wells appel/Group Melvin Design; fig 10. Piano Man, by Sikora Wells appel/Group Melvin Design; fig. 11. Light towers, by Sikora Wells appel/Group Melvin Design fig. 12. Green towers, by Sikora Wells appel/Group Melvin Design; fig. 13. A community-based process, by PhilaNOMA;

ACKNOWLEDGEMENTS: The author gratefully acknowledges Temple University for its generous support of her research, presentation and publication of this work through a Summer Research Grant. This article was originally published in the 2016 ACSA International Conference | CROSS AMERICAS Probing Disglobal Networks Proceedings.

WE ARE NEVER NOT INSIDE

Image Credits_ fig. 01_ Daniel Koehler, AD Research Cluster 8; fig. 02, 03 courtesy by the author: fig. 04_ Mark Foster Gage Architects; fig. 05_ Daniel Koehler, AD Research Cluster 8.

KLAN KOSOVA

Name of project_ Klan KOSOVA Television; Location_ Pristina, Kosovo; Name of design firm_ ANARCH; Name(s) of key architects/designers_ Astrit NIXHA; project assistant_ Artan HOXHA; Name of owner_ Klan Kosova; Name of consultants_ Xero A; Name of contractor_ ASHALA; Name of photographer_ Valdrin REXHAJ and Astrit NIXHA; Year completed_ February 2015; Website address of design firm_ www. anarch.biz; Image Credits_ Valdrin REXHAJ and Astrit NIXHA.

THE PAST EMBODIED IN ACTION

Name of project_ Cattedrale di Pozzuoli; Location_ Pozzuoli, Napoli, Italy; Name(s) of key architects/designers_ Marco Dezzi Bardeschi (Capogruppo), Gnosis Architettura (Francesco Buonfantino, Antonio De Martino e Rossella Traversari), Alessandro Castagnaro, Renato De Fusco e Laura Gioeni; Name of owner_ Regione Campania; Name of structural engineer_ Giampiero Martuscelli; Electrical_ Domenico Trisciuoglio; HVAC_ Fulvio Capuano; Consultants_ Alessandra Angeloni (geologist), Mario Bencivenni (restoration history and theory), Giovanni Coppola (art historian and archaeologist), Sabino Giovannoni (conservationist), Ugo Grazioso (liturgist), Giorgio Piccinato (town planning), Furio Sacchi (archaeologist), Ferdinando Zaccheo (restoration specialist); Name of contractor_ Rione Terra Pozzuoli Consortium; Year completed_ 2014; Image Credits_ courtesy by Marco Dezzi Bardeschi

BIBIOGRAPHY:

-Lecoq, J., Carasso J.G., Lallias J.C. *The Moving Body: Teaching Creative Theatre*. 2nd Ed. London & New York: Bloomsbury, 2002.

-Pallasmaa, J. *The Eyes of the Skin: Architecture and the Senses*. Hoboken: Wiley, 2005.

-Pallasmaa, J. *The Thinking Hand: Existential and Embodied Wisdom in Architecture*. Hoboken: Wiley, 2009.

-Wittgenstein, L. *Culture and Value: A Selection from the Posthumous Remains*. 2nd Ed. Oxford & Malden: Blackwell Publishers, 1998.

FREE SPEECH COMES HOME

Name of project_ La Casa del Hijo Ahuizote; Location_ Ciudad de Mexico, Mexico; Name(s) of key architects/designers: Giacomo Castagnola (industrial designer); Name of owner_ Centro Documental Flores Magón, A.C.; Name of photographer_ fig. 01_ Roberto Arellano; all other images courtesy by the author; Website address of design firm_ http://giacomocastagnola.com/

EMPOWERING ACTIONS

Image Credits_ fig. 01, 02, 04 courtesy of Lilithphoto ©; fig. 03 by Sara Ceraolo.

BIBLIOGRAPHY:

-Agamben, Giorgio. *Homo Sacer: Sovereign Power and Bare Life*. Stanford, Calif: Stanford University Press, 1998.

-Campagnaro, Cristian and Valentina Porcellana. *Beauty, Participation and Inclusion.* In Art and Intercultural Dialogue. Comparative and International Education (A Diversity of Voices), edited by Susana Gonçalves and Suzanne Majhanovich, 217-31. Rotterdam: SensePublishers, 2016.

-Foucault, Michel. *Of Other Spaces*, translated by Jay Miskowiec. *Diacritics* 16, No. 1 : 22-27, 1968.

-Jonas, Wolfgang. *Design Research and its Meaning to the Methodological Development of the Discipline*. In *Design Research Now*. Board of International Research in Design, edited by Ralf Michel, 187-206. Basel: Birkhäuser, 2007.

-Marrone, Gianfranco. *Corpi sociali. Processi comunicativi e semiotica del testo*. Torino: Einaudi, 2007.

-Miller, Daniel. *Stuff*. Cambridge-UK, Malden-USA: Polity Press,. ePub, 2010.

-Van Aken, Mauro. *Introduzione*. In *Antropologia*: Annuario 5, No. 5 (2005): 5-13.

BEING, ARCHITECTURE AND ACTION

Image Credits_ Martin Heidegger_ www.renaud-camus.net/librairie/; Site de Renaud Camus : bio-bibliographie, journal, Le Jour ni l'Heure, chronologie, livres & textes en ligne (librairie/bookshop), site du château de Plieux (histoire, description, conditions de visite), tableaux, etc.; (CC BY-SA 2.0);

Hannah Arendt_ https://commons.wikimedia.org/wiki/File:PikiWiki_Israel_7706_Hannah_Senesh.jpg; Unknown (https://commons.wikimedia.org/wiki/File:PikiWiki_Israel_7706_Hannah_Senesh.jpg), „PikiWiki Israel 7706 Hannah Senesh", color adjustment, cropping by Int|AR, https://creativecommons.org/publicdomain/zero/1.0/legalcode

Eyal Weizman: Ekaterina Izmestieva (https://commons.wikimedia.org/wiki/File:Eyal_Weizman.jpg), „Eyal Weizman", color adjustment, cropping by Int|AR, https://creativecommons.org/licenses/by/2.0/legalcode

Georges-Eugène Haussmann: Unknown. Stitch and restoration by Jebulon (https://commons.wikimedia.org/wiki/File:Georges-Eugène_Haussmann_-_BNF_Gallica.jpg), „Georges-Eugène Haussmann - BNF Gallica", color adjustment, cropping by Int|AR, https://creativecommons.org/publicdomain/zero/1.0/legalcode

Le Corbusier: https://www.flickr.com/photos/27608953@N06/3200164455/in/album-72157605573066252/; Arquitecto Le Corbusier en su despacho; (CC BY-SA 2.0)

Roland Barthes_ https://www.flickr.com/photos/alyletteri/5352054723; Attribution 2.0 Generic (CC BY 2.0)

BIBLIOGRAPHY:

-Arendt, Hannah. *The Human condition*, University of Chicago Press, 1998.

-Ballantyne, Andrew. *Deleuze and Guattari for architects*. Routledge, 2008.

-De Certeau, Michel. *The practice of everyday life*. University of California Press, 1984.

-Hays, K. Michael. *Architecture Theory since 1968*. Columbia Books for Architecture, 2000.

-Heidegger, Martin. *Building Dwelling Thinking*, 1951.

-Segal, Rafi and Eyal Weizman. *A civilian occupation, the politics of Israeli architecture*, Babel Verso, 2003.

APPROPRIATING ARCHITECTURE

Image Credits_ fig.01_ *Greenpeace UN Climate Projection*, 2014, copyright: Greenpeace; fig. 02_ *Greenpeace Planet Earth First Projection*, 2017, copyright: Greenpeace; fig. 03_ *Greenpeace Planet Earth First Projection*, 2017, Greenpeace; fig. 04_ *Planet Earth First Projection*, 2017, copyright: Team Vulvarella; fig. 05_ Team Vulvarella, US Embassy Berlin, March 8, 2017 *Planet Earth First Projection*, 2017, copyright: Team Vulvarella; fig. 06_ Drury live in the subway, Berlin, 2017, copyright Michael Ang; fig. 07_ Shamsia Hassani, *Dream Graffiti*, 2015, copyright Shamsia Hassani; fig. 08_ Shamsia Hassani, *Dream Graffiti*, 2015, copyright Shamsia Hassani.

THE ELEPHANT REFUGE

Name of project_ The Elephant Refuge in Rejmyre; Location_ Rejmyre, Sweden; Name of design firm_ atelier Kristoffer Tejlgaard; Name of key architects/designers_ Kristoffer Tejlgaard; Name of owner_ Daniel Pelz and Kristoffer Tejlgaard; Name of photographer_ Kristoffer Tejlgaard; Year completed_ 2018 (Design Proposal); Website address of design firm_ https://www.instagram.com/ktejlgaard/; Image credit_ Kristoffer Tejlgaard.

UNDER THE RADAR

Interview conducted by Elizabeth Debs and Liliane Wong; Interviewee_ Joe Garlick; Image Credits_ fig. 01, 02, 04, 06 by Elizabeth Debs; fig. 03, 05 by Liliane Wong.

SECOND ACT

Name of project_ Mercado de Xabregas; Location_ Lisbon, Portugal; Construction Area_ 2837.18m2; Date_ 2016/2017; Owner_ AR.CO - CENTRO DE ARTE E COMUNICAÇÃO VISUAL; Designer_ SANTA-RITA ARQUITECTOS, João Santa-Rita; Collaborators_ Pedro Guedes Lebre; Artur Simões Dias; Carolina Portugal; João Vidal Sousa; Structures_ Teixeira Trigo, Lda; Eng. João Leite Garcia; Other Engineering and Systems_ GRAUCELCIUS, CONSULTORES DE ENGENHARIA, GESTÃO E PLANEAMENTO, LDA, Eng. Carlos Oliveira; Construction Supervisor_ TEIXEIRA TRIGO, LDA; Eng. João Cordeiro; Contractor_ GUALDIM NUNES DA SILVA, LDA. Eng. Bruno Ribeiro; Photographer_ Inês Guedes Lebre; Image Credits_ fig. 01, fig. 06, fig. 8, fig.10 by IInês Navarro Soeiro Guedes Lebre; fig. 02 -05, fig 07, fig. 09 by ar.co, Centro de Arte & Comuniçâto Cisual, copyright_ Nuno Martinho.

COLOPHON

Kristina Anilane is a Ph.D. candidate at the department of Critical Studies and Creative Industries at Kingston School of Art researching emerging global urban initiative and formats of its curatorial implications. Her exhibitions and research projects including Imagine Moscow exhibition at the Design Museum London and Late Light project at Goldfinger House, in partnership with the National Trust UK. She holds Curating Contemporary Design MA from Kingston University and Design Museum. Kristina acts as creative director for Vesta 3D and is a co-founder for PROLETKINO independent platform for distribution, research and curatorial practice.

Cristian Campagnaro, is an Architect and Associate Professor at the Department of Architecture and Design of Polytechnic of Turin. He focuses his research on two topics: "Ecodesign and sustainable processes" toward a reduction of ecological footprint on the territories and populations; "Design for social inclusion and cohesion" via participatory, creative and interdisciplinary processes. He is co-responsible with Valentina Porcellana (University of Turin) of the action research "Living in the dorm" aimed to develop new product, process and system strategies to strength services for homeless adults.

Stefano Corbo is an architect, researcher and Assistant Professor at RISD (Rhode Island School of Design). He holds a PhD and an M.Arch. II in Advanced Architectural Design from UPM-ETSAM Madrid. Stefano has contributed to several international journals and has published two books: *From Formalism to Weak Form*. The Architecture and Philosophy of Peter Eisenman (Routledge, 2014), and *Interior Landscapes. A Visual Atlas* (Images, 2016). In 2012, Stefano founded his own office SCSTUDIO, a multidisciplinary network practicing architecture and design, preoccupied with the intellectual, economical and cultural context.

Elizabeth Debs is a studio critic in the Department of Interior Architecture at RISD. Debs received her Masters of Architecture form Harvard University, Graduate School of Design and a Bachelor of Art in Philosophy from Vassar College. Prior to joining the department in 2015, Debs worked for many years in the community development sector in Florida and Rhode Island. She is part of the Advisory Group for the AIA Housing Knowledge Community and promotes social equity as an important foundation in design studies. Debs has coordinated the INTAR department charrette, which pairs the talents of RISD with the needs of a community partner.

Nicolò Di Prima is Research Fellow at the Department of Architecture and Design of Polytechnic of Turin. His research focuses on design and cultural anthropology. He is currently working on interdisciplinary research projects dealing with participatory design processes in deep marginality contexts. He has conducted three academic workshop for the Bachelor's degree in Design and Visual Communication (Polytechnic of Turin) focused on co-design and social design issues.

Laura Gioeni is an architect, philosopher, independent researcher and lecturer. She initially trained at the School of Mimodrama in Milan, experiencing Jacques Lecoq's theatrical pedagogy, then graduated cum laude in both Architecture and Philosophy. She worked as architect, in the field of architectural design and adaptive reuse, and as adjunct professor at the Polytechnic of Milan. In 2017 she received the Italian National Scientific Qualification as associate professor in Architectural Design. Author of various books and essays, she is currently a secondary school teacher, engaged in theoretical research on the philosophy of architecture and in promoting mimodynamic methods in architectural education.

Sally Harrison is a Professor of Architecture and Head of the Master of Architecture Program in the Tyler School of Art of Temple University. Her design and scholarship addresses reemerging postindustrial neighborhoods as sites for social justice, creativity and learning. The work has been widely published in books and academic journals and has been recognized in national, international and regional design awards programs. Professor Harrison is the leader of The Urban Workshop, (http://tyler.temple.edu/urban-workshop-0) an interdisciplinary university-based design and research collaborative. Ms. Harrison received her Master of Architecture from MIT.

Heinrich Hermann earned master's degrees from the University of Applied Arts Vienna and Cornell, and his PhD from Harvard. Aside from RISD, he taught at Cornell, Montana State, Virginia Tech, Washington University in St. Louis, Harvard, Roger Williams, and Northeastern Universities, and from 2012-15 implemented SUNY's only BArch program, as chair and professor of architecture at SUNY Alfred State. He practiced in Austria, Germany, and Greater Boston with large and small firms, and through Hermann Design Studio in Concord, MA. With Liliane Wong and Markus Berger he co-founded the Int|AR Journal.

Dorothée King is the head of the Art Education department at the Art and Design Academy in Basel, Switzerland. She was in 2017 lecturer for the Department of Interior Architecture and HAVC at the Rhode Island School of Design. Her scholarship and teaching is invested in contemporary and modern art history, participatory exhibiting, immersive environments, ephemeral materials, and multisensory aesthetic experience. Her research has been published in her first monograph (*KUNST RIECHEN!* Athena-Verlag: Oberhausen 2016), in peer-review journals, and in edited volumes. After studying art, design, and media theory in Denmark, Germany and England, Dorothée King earned her PhD Berlin University of the Arts. She works internationally as a researcher, consultant and curator.

Fabia Mendoza is a Film and Art Director from Berlin Germany. Her first movie 'The White House Documentary', 75min, 2017 won at the 18th Beverly Hills Filmfestival 2018. Over the past 6 years she collaborated on a variety of projects including 'Another Pussy for Putin'- an act of solidarity art performance for the Russian punk band The Pussy Riots, 2012, and 'Amerikkka', a photo project in collaboration with Erica Garner, the daughter of the late Eric Garner. Fabia's photographic and cinematographic work have been featured by *Vogue Italia, Interview Magazine, ID magazine, CNN Style, Vanity Fair* among others. Her video and documentary material has been featured by BBC World, Arte, ZDF, CNN, etc.

Ryan Mendoza is an American artist who lives and works in Sicily and Berlin. He is the artist behind *The White House* (2015), the *Invitation* (2016), and the *Rosa Parks House Project* (2017). Primarily a painter, Ryan's artistic projects move between expressionism and realism, engaging Americana and historical reference. Ryan's work often depicts obsessive scenes, illustrating questions of hypocrisy and repression. Ryan has shown with a range of European galleries and museums including White Cube, London, Galerie Lelong, Paris and Museo Madre, Naples. He is the author of *Tutto e mio*, published in Italian (Everything is Mine) 2015, Bompiani.

Astrit Nixha graduated at faculty of Architecture, University of Pristina, Kosova. With over 25 years of architectural and managerial experience he runs the architectural office ANARCH, that he founded in 2004. His original experimental architecture, especially in adaptive reuse, presents cutting edge 21st century design principles of reduce, recycle and reuse. He is the recipient of several International project awards.

Clay Odom is Assistant Professor in the Interior Design Program at The University of Texas School of Architecture, a graduate of Texas Tech University's College of Architecture and the Columbia University Graduate School of Architecture Planning and Preservation, and a licensed Interior Designer. He is principal of the research-oriented design practice, studio MODO based in Austin, Texas. Clay's active practice in combination with his academic position are the platforms for design-based scholarship which leverages advanced design and fabrication to explore spatial, atmospheric and material effects generation in relation to objects and interiors.

Luis Sacristan Murga is a practicing Architect at Heatherwick Studio in London, where he has been working since 2015 on several international projects, including the new Google campus in California. He received his architectural education from several universities including the Polytechnic School of Madrid in Spain, Lunds Tekniska Högskola in Sweden and Rhode Island School of Design in the USA. He serves as a guest critic at the Architectural Association and he has been a teaching collaborator in Diploma 17 organizing design workshops and reviewing student theses. Through the principles of adaptive reuse and the use of public space, Sacristan Murga works to understand the ways in which architecture can transform consciousness and merge with nature.

João Santa Rita is the founding partner of Santa-Rita Arquitectos. Since 1998, he is Associate Professor at the Universidade Autónoma de Lisboa. In 2005, he was an invited Member of the Akademie Fur Baukultur and from 2014/2016 the President of the Portuguese Chamber of Architects. His work and his drawings have been extensively exhibited in Europe, South America and the US. He was nominated for the Mies Van der Rohe Prize in 2012.

João José Santos holds a B. Arch and M. Arch from Escola Superior Artística do Porto and he is currently living and working from Berlin. He is specialized in not being specialized as he is moved by arbitrary challenges and mundane curiosity over science and art realms. He independently expresses this himself by exercising, on various mediums, over artifacts about space and the human condition. He continuously looks for opportunities to rationally and physically assist on consequential projects and interventions.

Enrique Aureng Silva received his Bachelor of Architecture from Universidad Nacional Autónoma de México (UNAM), a Master in Critical Conservation at Harvard GSD and has practiced architecture in Mexico and the US. His research focuses on the intervention, transformation and reuse of historic buildings in Latin America, especially in post-disaster scenarios. He is editor of *Oblique*, Open Letters and Platform XI. When not thinking architecture or editing texts, he writes fiction in the form of short stories.

Barbara Stehle is an art and architecture historian, educator, writer, art advisor and curator. She holds a PHD from the Sorbonne and has worked for several museums including the Pompidou Center and The Zurich Kunsthaus. She has written extensively on modern and contemporary arts and architecture. In 2014 she gave a Ted x talk "Architecture as a tool for Human Investigation in the case of the Cambodian Genocide". Stehle has taught at Columbia University, RISD and NYU before founding "Art Intelligentsia", her own heterotopia.

Diogo Vale is deeply interested in breaking the boundaries of the architecture profession, with an intense curiosity in the meaning of preservation in the XXI century, and the studying of architecture as a tool for social intervention. Diogo attained a Bachelor and Master in Architecture at the ESAP (Escola Superior de Arquitectura do Porto) in Porto, Portugal and has worked as a Carpenter/Performer/Artist/Architect. He is currently living in Berlin Germany where he works as an Artist Assistant and Architecture consultant in Studio Mendoza as one of the architects/coordinators of the *Rosa Parks House Project*.

EDITORS

Ernesto Aparicio is a Senior Critic in the Department of Graphic Design at RISD. Aparicio earned his BA at the Escuela de Bellas Artes, La Plata, Buenos Aires and completed his Post Graduate Studies at the Ecole des Art Decoratifs, Paris. Prior to moving to the US, he served as Art Director for Editions du Seuil in Paris, while maintaining his own graphic design practice, Aparicio Design Inc. Best known for his work in the world of publishing, Aparicio has worked on corporate identities, publications, and way-finding for corporations and institutions in France, Japan, and the US. Recently, Aparicio was named Creative Director for the New York firm DFA.

Markus Berger is Associate Professor and Graduate Program Director in the Department of Interior Architecture at RISD. Berger holds a Diplomingenieur für Architektur from the Technische Universität Wien, Austria and is a registered architect (SBA) in the Netherlands. Prior to coming to the US, Berger practiced and taught in the Netherlands, Austria, India, and Pakistan, and currently heads his own art and design studio in Providence. His work, research, writing, and teaching focus on art and design interventions in the built environment, including issues of historic preservation, sensory experience and alteration. He is a co-founder and co-editor of the *Int|AR Journal*.

Nick Heywood is a designer, educator and writer. He received his Masters of Interior Architecture from the Rhode Island School of Design, where he also completed his B.F.A. He is a critic in the Interior Architecture department at RISD and acts as an advisor to students on writing within the thesis cycle. He teaches art and design courses at the University of Rhode Island and is on the board of two nonprofit organizations devoted to architectural preservation. His writing focuses on protection of threatened historic sites and proposed public policy, with an interest in the relationship between sustainable practice and historic preservation.

Liliane Wong is Professor and Head of the Department of Interior Architecture at RISD. Wong received her Masters of Architecture from Harvard University, Graduate School of Design and a Bachelor of Art in Mathematics from Vassar College. She is a registered Architect in Massachusetts and has practiced in the Boston area, including in her firm, MWA. She is the author of *Adaptive Reuse_Extending the Lives of Buildings*, co-author of *Libraries: A Design Manual* and contributing author of *Designing Interior Architecture and Flexible Composite Materials in Architecture, Construction and Interiors*. A long time volunteer at soup kitchens, she emphasizes the importance of public engagement in architecture and design in her teaching. Wong is a co-founder and co-editor of the *Int|AR Journal*.

MDES Interior Studies [Adaptive Reuse]

The 2+ year Master of Design (MDes) in Interior Studies [Adaptive Reuse] provides a unique design education on the alteration of existing structures through interior interventions and adaptive reuse. The program establishes a clear aesthetic, theoretical and technological framework for the study of interior studies and adaptive reuse. Graduating students are properly equipped to engage in this subject in the general design field and to develop strategies in their work which recognize the importance of social and environmental responsibility.

MDES Interior Studies [Exhibition & Narrative Environments]

The study of Exhibition and Narrative Environments has been a part of the studio offerings of the Department of Interior Architecture for many years. The department has hosted annual studios specific to the design of the narrative environment that featured collaborations with the key members of the RISD Museum, the RISD Departments of Graphic Design, History of Art & Visual Culture and Brown University, in particular, the Haffenreffer Museum and the John Nicholas Brown Center. The Exhibition and Narrative Environments track consists of an MDes curriculum supported by courses offered in these other disciplines, formalizing the existing relationships with these departments.

MA Adaptive Reuse

Formerly called "MA Interior Architecture [ADAPTIVE REUSE]", the purpose of the Master of Arts (MA) in Adaptive Reuse is to provide a unique specialist design education on the subject of adaptive reuse as a post-professional study to a first degree in Architecture. The program aims to establish a clear aesthetic, theoretical and technological framework for the study of adaptive reuse, in order that graduating students are properly equipped to engage in the practice of working with existing buildings, structures and spaces. It enables students to develop strategies in their work which recognize the importance of social and environmental responsibility.

BFA Interior Studies [Adaptive Reuse]

The BFA is centered on rethinking the life of existing spaces – through design alterations, renovations and adaptive reuse, but encompasses also a very wide range of studies that engage with existing fabric, from installation design and retail design to more traditional interior design.

Please find our current call for papers on our website.

http://intar-journal.risd.edu/

Previous published volumes of Int|AR

Vol. **01 "Inaugural Issue"**
2009, (out of print)
co-editors: Markus Berger, Heinrich Hermann and Liliane Wong

Vol. **02 "Adapting Industrial Structures"**
2011, ISBN: 978-0-9832723-0-4
co-editors: Markus Berger, Heinrich Hermann and Liliane Wong

Vol. **03 "Emerging Economies"**
2012, ISBN: 978-0-9832723-1-1
co-editors: Markus Berger, Liliane Wong
Associate Editor Maya Marx

Vol. **04 "Difficult Memories: Reconciling Meaning"**
2013, ISBN: 978-0-9832723-2-8
co-editors: Markus Berger, Liliane Wong

Vol. **05 "Resilience and Adaptability"**
2014, ISBN 978-3-03821-606-3
co-editors: Markus Berger, Liliane Wong
Special Editor: Damian White

Vol. **06 "The Experience Economy"**
2015 ISBN:978-3-03821-984-2
co-editors: Markus Berger, Liliane Wong
Special Editor:Jeffrey Katz

Vol. **07 "Art in Context"**
2016 ISBN:978-3-0356-0834-2
co-editors: Markus Berger, Liliane Wong
Special Editor: Patricia Philips

Vol. **08 "Water as Catalyst"**
2017 ISBN:978-3-0356-1197-7
co-editors: Markus Berger, Liliane Wong